STUDIES IN SOCIAL POLICY AND WELFARE, X

Process and Structure in
Higher Education

Studies in Social Policy and Welfare
Edited by R. A. Pinker

In the same series

Process and Structure in Higher Education

Tony Becher
Professor of Education,
University of Sussex

and

Maurice Kogan
Professor of Government and Social Administration,
Brunel University

HEINEMANN · LONDON

Heinemann Educational Books Ltd
22 Bedford Square, London WC1B 3HH

LONDON EDINBURGH MELBOURNE AUCKLAND
HONG KONG SINGAPORE KUALA LUMPUR NEW DELHI
IBADAN NAIROBI JOHANNESBURG
EXETER (NH) KINGSTON PORT OF SPAIN

British Library Cataloguing in Publication Data

Becher, Tony
    Process and structure in higher education. —
    (Studies in social policy and welfare; 10).
    1. Education, Higher — Great Britain
    I. Title   II. Kogan, Maurice   III. Series
    378.41   LA636.8

    ISBN 0-435-82507-0

Typeset by The Castlefield Press of High Wycombe
in 11/12pt Baskerville, and printed in Great Britain by
Fakenham Press Ltd, Fakenham, Norfolk

Contents

Preface

This book leaves its authors in debt to many friends and colleagues. It began with a collaborative effort undertaken with Jack Embling to produce our *Systems of Higher Education: United Kingdom* (1978) for the International Council for Educational Development. Both that study and the succeeding stages which led to the writing of this book were encouraged by Sir Fred Dainton, then Chairman of the University Grants Committee, and funded by a grant from the Leverhulme Trust.

Throughout our study we have been fortunate enough to find ourselves part of a network which has helpfully commented on our writing as it has developed. We were particularly helped by Professor Margaret Archer, University of Warwick; Mrs Ann Bone, North East London Polytechnic; Lord Boyle, Leeds University; Geoffrey Caston, then Registrar, University of Oxford; Dr Clive Church, University of Lancaster; Dr Hendrik Gideonse, University of Cincinnatti; Professor John Honey, Syracuse University; Dr Jan-Erik Lane, Umea University; Professor Jack Meadows, University of Leicester; Dr Barbara Nelson, Massachusetts Institute of Technology; Dr Malcolm Parlett, Education Development Center, Boston; Professor Robert Pinker, London School of Economics and Political Science; Mr Rune Premfors, University of Stockholm; Mr Peter Scott, *Times Higher Education Supplement*; Dr Geoffrey Squires, University of Hull; Professor Martin Trow, Berkeley University; and Dr Robert Woodbury, University of Massachusetts.

One of the most pleasant aspects of our project has been a developing friendship with many Swedish scholars and administrators, most of whom gathered at a conference arranged by the Swedish National Board of Universities and Colleges at Dalaro, Sweden, in June 1978. The paper[1] which we gave to that conference forms the substance of Chapters 2 and 6 of this book. We should especially like to identify Dr Eskil Bjorklund, Director of Research at the National Board of Universities and Colleges, who has done so much to encourage studies of higher education in Sweden and elsewhere.

Sally Harris has both typed the successive manuscripts and administered our project. This book could not have been written without her.

Tony Becher
Maurice Kogan

[1] Tony Becher and Maurice Kogan, 'Process and structure in the higher education system', in *Research in Higher Education*, Swedish National Board of Universities and Colleges, 1979.

1. Introduction

The Boundaries of our Territory
Higher education in the United Kingdom now accommodates well over half a million students at any given time. Over the years it has helped to shape the destinies of many of the nation's most able men and women. It is assumed to be a force for the fairer distribution of educational and vocational opportunity throughout the population. It takes up a discernible share of the national budget. It also helps in the production of the country's wealth through the training it provides in specialized skills and through the contribution it makes to research and the advancement of technology.

These are all good reasons for taking higher education seriously. Any one of them could well justify a new addition to the existing literature on the subject. However, we had a different consideration in view in writing this book: namely, the intrinsic interest of the higher education system and of its diverse and distinct components. We decided from the outset to concentrate our attention on how the workings of the enterprise as a whole could best be understood and explained, not in terms of some extrinsic rationale but in and for itself.

The book is explicitly limited as to both time and place. That is to say, it concerns the academic scene in contemporary Britain, rather than higher education in other parts of the world, or in the past or future. This relatively restricted framework reflects our own direct familiarity with the subject-matter. We have nevertheless been concerned to avoid taking a narrowly parochial view. Our discussions are set against a historical background in Chapter 2. There are references at a number of relevant places throughout the text to other national systems (and particularly those of the USA and Sweden, with which we are the most familiar). Finally, in

Chapter 10, we move outside higher education to explore the implications of our work for the analysis of other major sectors of public policy.

Since our main concern is not with the description of the existing state of affairs, but with the clarification of basic structures and the illumination of underlying processes, we would in any case expect our analysis to have a wider currency than the specific here and now from which it happens to have been developed. The essential elements which go to make up a system of higher education — the individual teachers and students, the departments and other basic units, the component institutions, the central agencies for management and control — do not differ dramatically from one point to another in the history of Britain in the past generation, or even from one point to another in the geography of the advanced countries at the present time. Nor do the relationships, tensions and divergencies between those various elements change or fluctuate in a way which would preclude any meaningful generalization. Of course there are important differences — for example, between systems with centralized and decentralized forms of control — and we do not wish to deny these, or to argue them out of existence. We shall take it as our main task, however, to explore points of commonality rather than to dwell on points of contrast.

Purposes and Audiences
The main virtue of seeking to identify fundamental components and interconnections is that if the effort is successful it has a wider relevance and a more enduring validity than the more literal depiction of the contemporary scene. But this strategy must by its nature disappoint those with other expectations of a study of British higher education — and especially those who prefer topographical to topological description.

The contrast may be illustrated by noting some distinctions between a detailed street map of London and a London Transport map of the underground system. The latter is a drastic simplification of reality, with all detail pruned away except that portraying the intercommunication between different stations. Even distances and directions are ignored in the interests of topological simplicity and clarity. To anyone needing to find his or her way round the underground railways, it is a superbly efficient device (as anyone who has struggled to follow the topographically realistic map of the Paris *metro* will readily acknowledge). But for someone wanting to trace a route on foot or by surface transport, the underground map is useless — only a map which accurately represents distances and directions, with accompanying details of street names and landmarks, will do. That in its turn, however, while it may portray all the relevant stations (and even perhaps the routes), is for the underground traveller a poor substitute for the map of the tube.

This book sets out to be more like a London underground map than a street plan. With that said, it remains to answer the question what kind of audience it seeks to attract. Although authors are not necessarily the best judges in this regard, it seems a fair guess that our main readership will fall into three main categories: intellectuals with a particular set of interests; administrators and politicians at various levels; and students of public policy.

The first of these audiences — whom we have labelled intellectuals — comprises those readers who (like ourselves) find some fascination in the higher education system and want to understand its workings better — either because they have at some time passed through it, or because they are participants in some capacity within it. For them, perhaps, the main appeal of the book will lie in the exploration of differing values between different components in the academic enterprise, the characteristic ways in which standards are monitored and resources distributed, and the nature and limits of change within the system.

The second audience — of administrators and politicians — is one which we would much like to interest in our analysis. We believe that the difficulty, from the standpoint of a central agency or even from the level of the institution as a whole, of appreciating the dominant norms of individuals or departments, has been responsible for many wasteful, frustrating, ineffective and counter-productive attempts to institute new policies. There is a pressing need, on this argument, to bridge the gap between an understanding of the macro-structure of higher education and an ability to comprehend its micro-structure. Sound governance lies in knowing and taking due account of the tribal customs in the hinterland, not in brushing them aside or trampling them underfoot. If this book succeeds in helping to promote more sensitive management of the system and its components, we shall be very well satisfied.

Finally, both of us have an academic and professional interest in advancing the study of public policy: and we hope that the present work will accomplish something useful towards that end. We recognize that higher education is not usually thought of in the context of social administration, and that it might strike some people as odd that our book appears as one of a series devoted to that theme.

There is no need to justify the case in detail here, since the rest of the book will do it for us. For the moment, it must suffice to say that those engaged in study within the broad field of government, the social services, public institutions and policy analysis, should find a number of the ideas developed in this book to be of direct relevance to their own thinking. This is particularly so at a time when British social policy research includes some of the leading contributions to the understanding of how institutions work and what their impact is on those within and outside them.[1] We would expect students and scholars in this domain to be able (if they so wished) to take over and adapt to their particular needs the framework of analysis set out in Chapter 2, as well as the general techniques exemplified in Chapters 4 to 7 of identifying values, relating them to operations and exploring the constraints imposed by institutional structures. The final chapter suggests more specific ways in which this translation might be made.

The Nature and Origins of our Approach

It may be helpful at this point to say something about our methodological stance. The scientific paradigm has so successfully dominated social inquiry over the last half-century that any other approach is taken to demand an explanation, if not an apology. While we see no need for the second, we accept the obligation, in departing from strongly entrenched methodology, to put forward a more careful account of our rationale and our approach than would be expected of any staunchly positivistic and empirically based inquiry.

Our readiness to do so is reinforced by the puzzled concern of one or two sympathetically interested colleagues on reading parts of the text in draft — and especially Chapter 2, setting out the framework of our analysis. What, we were asked, was the basis of our choosing the framework we did? Well, it seemed to fit, and to help make sense of, the situations we wanted to discuss. But where, the interrogation continued, did it *come* from? Out of our heads, we supposed. Oh, that wasn't a serious answer, surely, since it would completely undermine its validity: there must be some testable base for the model. Did we derive or modify it from other people's empirical findings? What were our references? Or did we reach it by induction from a series of instances of higher education systems?

It would be misleading to pretend to the degree of scientific respectability which our well-wishing inquisitors expected to find in our approach. It derives, fundamentally, from a different intellectual tradition, namely, that of analytical philosophy and its associated procedures of conceptual clarification. We take ourselves — at least in terms of our defining framework — as developing a structure of thought within which it is possible to organize, and ultimately better to understand, the complex world of higher education. We are not here in the business of discovering new facts. All our readers will be familiar with some of our assertions and some may be familiar with all of them. It is the way of looking at the phenomena, rather than the phenomena themselves, for which we would claim some originality.

Still, it might be objected, if we are offering no new facts, but only a new theory to account for those facts, the theory itself must be either true or false: we cannot so easily escape the inexorable rule of empiricism. Once again, to say this is to push our work into an inappropriate mould. We are not offering theories about higher education, in the sense of law-like propositions which have predictive (and hence falsifiable or verifiable) properties. We are attempting, rather, to re-arrange the existing conceptual maps of higher education in such a way as to make more clearly evident interconnections, interrelationships and inherent properties which are in one sense already known but in another not adequately recognized. In saying this, we make no claim that the same material could not be organized and interpreted along a variety of different lines for a variety of different purposes (though it would remain appropriate to judge some interpretations as better, or worse, than others).

One straightforward example of the kind of conceptual mapping which we have in view can be found in the general domain of social policy. The notion of the single-parent family has come widely into currency in the last few years, linking together the previously separate (but individually familiar) phenomena of young widowed mothers — or fathers — with dependent children, divorced parents and what were previously called unmarried mothers. The new concept has underlined a previously neglected comparability — of the organizational and psychological stress created by coping with children in the absence of a spouse — at the expense of failing to separate the different subgroups in terms of social acceptability and moral praise and blame.

It would not, in this example, be appropriate to ask questions about truth or falsity, but only about the appropriateness of the concept to the situation, its usability and its degree of general acceptance. So too, in the case of the conceptual framework we develop in this book, we would readily accept its evaluation in terms of whether it seems to fit the domain under review, whether it helps to make it more readily intelligible and whether it can usefully be taken up and developed by others in the same or related contexts. Its status has to be judged, we would argue, as a good or bad conceptual interpretation, rather than as a correct or incorrect theory, of how the education system works.

With so much in the way of establishing the epistemological status of our framework, it is also possible — and may be thought relevant by some readers — to offer a brief historical account of its genesis and evolution. The main intellectual debt owed by the authors is — on the face of it — an unexpected one. Both of us were present at a conference organized by Ben Snyder, Director of the MIT Division for Study and Research in Education, and held in Oxford in March 1977. One of the circulated papers was a chapter from his then forthcoming book on the British Broadcasting Corporation by Tom Burns, Professor of

Sociology at Edinburgh University.[2] It brought out the sharp contrast — which seemed to most of the participants clearly applicable to higher education also — between what people were required in terms of their jobs to do and what those same people's own values, aspirations and loyalties were.

Reflection on this contrast (which was itself derived from a soundly based piece of empirical sociology) led to the development of two modes — the normative and the operational — as possible descriptors of conceptually distinct, though in practice interrelated, aspects of academic life. Once the two modes were sufficiently articulated to be applied to an analysis of higher education, it became increasingly clear that different levels of the system would need to be distinguished along a second dimension. The number of levels was determined at four because four sufficiently distinct clusters of values and operations could be discerned as between individuals, basic units, institutions and central authorities. If, in the event, we are challenged to say why we selected two modes of analysis and four levels of organization, we can offer no better reason than that they seemed to fit the case and to provide a conceptual framework which helped us (and we would hope others) to reach a clearer understanding of what we already knew.

Admittedly, we did not approach our analysis with empty minds. Both of us had some previous knowledge of the field of higher education: Tony Becher from his work with the Nuffield Higher Education Group (which involved a very detailed field study over the four years 1972–6 in all the British universities and most of the polytechnics); Maurice Kogan from his active research interests in educational policy-making and his direct involvement in the world of government and the sponsorship of research. The background understanding which we possessed about the system may well have helped us to avoid reaching premature conclusions based on our framework, and even to explore more rigorously than we could otherwise have done the extent to which it matched the phenomena. Nevertheless, the framework was not in any sense empirically derived: it was developed analytically to help us the better to organize our existing knowledge.

What the Reader Might Derive from this Book

This book, then, could be characterized in terms of an emphasis on conceptual clarification rather than description, a concern to link the macro-structure of higher education with its micro-structure, an involvement in policy analysis and the furtherance of sound policy-making, and an interest in trying to understand not only the differing value perspectives within academia as a whole, but also the ways in which acceptable resolutions can be reached between them.

In some of the following chapters we consider aspects of the historical background to British higher education, examine the nature and incidence of innovations within the system, and review the impact of evaluation, accountability and resource allocation procedures. We discuss these not as issues in their own right so much as elements necessary to a coherent understanding of the academic enterprise. Our approach to each such theme is of necessity limited, in being instrumental to a different end: it would be mistaken for a reader to expect to be presented with anything like a rounded picture of the topic in question.

Although we do not set out to look in any comprehensive way at the evolution of the system, or the occurrence of changes within it, or the mechanisms by which judgements are made and resources distributed, we do aspire to a reasonably thorough and self-contained examination of each of the four levels we have identified — namely, central authorities, institutions, basic units and individuals. Accordingly, a reader of any of the subject-specific chapters concerned (4 to 7) should — unlike the reader of any of the thematic chapters (3, 8 and 9) — come away with a fair idea of the norms and operations which characterize the particular level in question.

This contrast is made only to underline the differing functions, in the overall structure of the book, of subject-specific chapters and thematic chapters: it is not that we want particularly to encourage readers to sample, according to taste, the odd chapter here or there. The four levels serve as main elements in the explanation of how the system is articulated, and are therefore explored as subjects in themselves. The thematic chapters serve to underline and clarify the relationships between the various levels, and to show the system in a temporal perspective: it is through these chapters that we seek to convert a series of static camera-shots into an animated motion picture.

The nature and characteristics of the system as a whole, the way it works, some explanation of *why* it works in the way it does, and some insights into its component elements — all these form the subject-matter of Chapters 3 to 9. The remaining three chapters — 1, 2 and 10 — could be described as providing a surrounding frame. Chapter 2 presents the conceptual structure within which the subsequent analysis is carried out, and Chapter 10, as has already been remarked, explores the applicability of the approach to other areas of social policy.

What, then, could readers expect to gain by staying with us through the course of our exploration? We hope, first, that they will each acquire a new and clarifying conceptual lens through which to view that which is already familiar, and through which to make better sense of anything unfamiliar which comes into their field of vision; second, that they might be able to pick up, apply and develop further some of the subsidiary distinctions which we draw in our more detailed accounts of the different levels within the system; finally, that those who start with a prime interest in higher education may gain a somewhat wider perspective, seeing their subject as cognate with such other domains as health, social welfare and the like, while those who come from a social policy background may not only (with the others) acquire a usable conceptual framework, but also see it in action in a complex field whose characteristics are not far different from those of their own.

The achievement of the last objective depends on the successful delineation of the model or framework itself, and on the demonstration of its applicability to areas outside higher education. It is to the first of these twin tasks that we shall turn in our next chapter.

2. A Model for Higher Education

Introduction

It can sometimes be helpful, in explaining complex social and political phenomena, to refer to a deliberately simplified representation of those phenomena. There are no obvious rules for constructing such representations, and no standard means of checking their validity. Often one is left with nothing more satisfactory than a sense of a good fit, or of logical consistency, a feeling of appropriateness, a shock of recognition. Representations of reality in the social sciences may have certain features in common with striking caricatures, telling metaphors, or good interpretations of a play or a musical score. They highlight particular aspects of the whole, at the expense of others; but do so in such a way as to enhance understanding rather than to distort reality.

In this chapter we attempt to develop a portrayal of higher education which meets the requirement of simplifying and making more readily comprehensible while at the same time remaining true to reality. We have so far referred to representations and portrayals; but it is probably in the end easier to follow current usage and adopt the terminology of constructing or setting out a model.

The term 'model' has come to have a variety of different meanings. We shall employ it here in a non-technical sense, as a straightforward, but necessarily and deliberately simplified, set of categories for thinking about British higher education and looking at the relationships between its components. These categories, components and relationships can be compactly summarized in tabular form and it is the resulting figure to which we will refer as our model. We ascribe no special powers or properties to the model itself, other than those of conveniently presenting abstract ideas in concrete visual terms. It must, to be of any use, stand up to the test of being recognizable; it must succeed in reflecting without distortion important discontinuities in value; and above all it must provide a coherent and conceptually sound analysis of the complex phenomena of higher education.

We do not suggest that the model has predictive power of the kind offered by theories in the natural sciences; nor that it adequately incorporates the time dimension in a way that would make it a useful tool for the social historian. Our analysis relates to one particular decentralized system of higher education. It could be extended without much difficulty to other decentralized systems, or even (see Chapter 10) to somewhat more centralized public services within the British welfare state: but a significantly different kind of model, especially in terms of relationships between components, would need to be developed for strongly centralized countries. Finally, the model sets out to portray the characteristic features of institutions which are primarily concerned with teaching. The networks for predominantly research-based individuals and units would overlap with, but show structural properties which differ in various ways from, those we discuss below.

The Structural Levels in the System

We now turn to the business of assembling the model itself. In the discussions which follow we distinguish between four familiar elements in the structure of any higher education system. The first is the central level, involving the various national and local authorities who are between them charged with overall planning, resource allocation and the monitoring of standards. The second level is that of the individual institution, as defined in law (through its charters or instruments of governance) and by convention (through its various decision-making bodies).

We have called the third level the 'basic unit', because its precise nature varies between different institutions. In many traditional universities, it corresponds with subject-based departments; but in some newer ones the basic unit may be a more broadly constituted 'school of study'. In other institutions again, it may be defined by a course team — namely, an interdisciplinary group of teachers who collectively provide a major component of the undergraduate curriculum. The main characteristics of such basic units are that they have academic responsibility for an identifiable course or group of courses, that they have their own operating budgets (and some discretion in disposing of them) and that they exercise some element of choice in the recruitment of professional colleagues (and often also of students). They may in certain cases engage in collective research activities, but this is far from being a defining feature.

Finally, the system is composed of individuals: teaching staff, researchers, students, administrators and ancillary workers. We shall focus in our discussion mainly on the teachers, as in British higher education they normally play the main role in shaping academic, institutional and curricular policy, though we shall also give some attention to students.

In the first stage in the construction of the model, then, we have merely identified four elements representing the different structural levels within the system (Table 2.1).

Table 2.1 The structural components of the model

Individual	Basic unit	Institution	Central authority

Two considerations need to be emphasized in the interpretation of this part of the model. The first is that the elements are meant to represent functions rather than entities (to illustrate this, the same people may operate at some times as individual academics and at others as representing basic units; particular institutions can, in certain aspects of what they do, depart from their institutional role to act as central authorities, or even as basic units). The second consideration is that the fourfold categorization deliberately simplifies reality: the more complex components — and especially the central authority and the institution — will subsequently be seen to function in a variety of different styles and to embody a diverse collection of entities.

Two Modes, and the Development of a Matrix
The second stage in the process depends on a less familiar set of distinctions. It separates two components in the

everyday life of the academic world which are not in practice sharply distinguished. The first of these relates to the monitoring and maintenance of values within the system as a whole. It might be designated, briefly, as the normative mode. The second, in contrast, refers to the business of carrying out practical tasks at different levels within the system. It could be labelled as the operational mode.

Although these two modes obviously interact — and we shall go on, towards the end of this section, to discuss the nature of their interaction — their characteristics can be readily marked off one from another. Their inseparability in practice and clear differentiation in theory recall the familiar contrast between mind and body. Looked at in this light, the normative/operational distinction can be considered as denoting two aspects of the same state of affairs. The contrast between the one and the other is related to the difference between what people actually do — or what they are institutionally required to do — and what they count as important. The distinction also has some kinship with the familiar differences between fact and value and between everyday practice as defined by law and ideal practice as defined by morality. However, the best way to draw out the differences between the two modes is perhaps within the context of discussing the model itself in more detail.

Allowing still for a certain sketchiness in the delineation of the normative and operational components, we now have the basis of an eight-cell matrix which marks off the two modes in relation to each of the four structural components (Table 2.2).

Table 2.2 The eight elements of the model

	Individual	Basic unit	Institution	Central authority
Normative	1	2	3	4
Operational	5	6	7	8

The Cells of the Matrix
The next step must be to fill out the eight elements or cells of this matrix in sufficient detail to make it possible to discuss the interconnections between them. This task can

best be tackled by taking the eight numbered elements in turn and commenting on the nature and implications of each.

Normative Mode
(1) The main characteristics at the individual level in the normative mode are an emphasis on fulfilling personal wants and meeting personal expectations, linked with a general concern to maximize job satisfaction. These might be called intrinsic features of the element in question. However, there is also an extrinsic characteristic, in that most individuals derive some sense of support from the working group to which they belong, and reciprocate this by subscribing to the group's norms. (As we shall see, the combination of intrinsic and extrinsic features also occurs at the other levels of the system.)

(2) The basic unit, viewed in its normative mode, is mainly taken up with maintaining the group norms and values which give it its sense of coherence. It operates the collective credit system through which members of the immediate professional group, and the wider network of comparable groups in other institutions, obtain rewards, advancement and recognition. Thus, for example, a history department in a particular university is concerned to endorse the canons of historical scholarship and codes of good professional practice in the subject. In doing so, its own departmental reputation will be preserved and enhanced, and in addition its individual members may the more easily gain promotion in other history departments in other universities, whether at home or abroad. But at the same time, in the interests of survival, any such basic unit will also need to fall in with the extrinsic demands of the parent institution, which will not necessarily coincide with its own particular sectional concerns.

(3) Academic institutions are predominantly engaged, in their normative aspect, in setting and monitoring rules rather than in making substantive judgements of quality. In other words, their role emerges most clearly in the maintenance of 'due process', although they also have important developmental functions. They seek to ensure that the proper procedures are followed by basic units in relation to academic

appointments, the use of funds, the selection of students, the protocols of assessment and the like. Institutions as a whole do not normally lay down collective criteria for excellence. Rather, their tendency is to monitor the normative ambitions of basic units and to ensure that these conform to the shared interests of the group. In many higher education systems, institutions also have an extrinsic concern with meeting the requirements of central authorities, and of ensuring that the range of courses they provide matches the demands of applicants and employers.

(4) Just as academic institutions monitor their basic units, so too the central authorities have the normative task of monitoring the standards of their constituent institutions. They are also, however, expected to identify the extrinsic requirements on higher education of the economy and of society at large. Assuming that they succeed in this slippery task, they are then expected to perform the even more remarkable achievement of changing the system itself to match such requirements. Their possible means of doing so are reviewed in (8) below.

At this point, we might conveniently summarize the elements in the normative mode, as shown in Table 2.3.

Table 2.3 The elements in the normative mode

Individual	*Basic unit*	*Institution*	*Central authority*
Intrinsic: job satisfaction; personal wants and expectations	Intrinsic: maintaining peer group norms and values	Intrinsic: maintaining due academic process; initiating developments	Intrinsic: maintaining institutional standards
Extrinsic: subscription to group norms	Extrinsic: conformity with institutional requirements	Extrinsic: conformity to central demands	Extrinsic: meeting social and economic desiderata
(1)	(2)	(3)	(4)

Operational Mode
(5) Turning now to the operational mode, it is easy to see that at the individual level the main requirements are those of

occupational tasks. Such tasks are laid down mainly by the basic units, and comprise, for example, the teaching and/or research commitments of staff, and the learning demands and subsequent assessment exercises of students.

(6)   In operational terms, the key function of the basic unit is to define the actual nature and content of the unit's everyday practice. It is thus concerned mainly with issues of the curriculum, and in some cases also of research. It has to specify the working programme in sufficient detail to make it capable of implementation, and to translate the result in terms of individual tasks.

(7)   The institution has an important part to play in forward planning, and in implementing national or local policy decisions in return for the resources required for development. It is also concerned with the maintenance of established activities. It carries out these tasks mainly by the differential allocation of money and manpower between basic units.

(8)   The central authorities are operationally responsible for negotiating the recurrent funds made available for higher education by the legislature, and for allocating them between their constituent institutions. They are also in many cases charged with authorizing proposals for new developments or laying down specifications for new courses. By such means they can to a greater or lesser extent carry out their normative functions, as outlined in (4) above.[1]

A further summary is presented in Table 2.4.

Table 2.4 The elements in the operational mode

Individual	Basic unit	Institution	Central authority
Work required: research/ teaching, learning	Operating process: curriculum and/or research programme	Maintenance of institution; forward planning; implementing policy	Negotiation and allocation of central resources; sponsorship of new developments
(5)	(6)	(7)	(8)

Relationships Between Elements

Before this initial exploration of the model is completed, it remains to say something more about the relationships between adjacent elements in the matrix which we have just discussed. There are, of course, two sets of relationships: those which are horizontal (between elements 1 and 2, 2 and 3, and so on), and those which are vertical (between elements 1 and 5, 2 and 6, etc.). We shall look at them briefly in turn.

It has been implicit in our discussion of the normative mode that all the relevant relationships involve appraisal or judgement. Thus basic units relate normatively to individuals in terms of matching an individual's standards against the values of the group (elements 1 and 2). Institutions and basic units are linked in terms of procedural judgements in which the units must be seen to conform to institutional codes of practice (elements 2 and 3). National authorities carry out their monitoring function in relation to institutions by evaluating the general effectiveness of their basic units and by appraising their professional competence (elements 3 and 4).

In comparable ways, all the main relationships in the operational mode can be characterized in terms of the allocation of resources, responsibilities and tasks. The individual's activities are set out in terms of the operational requirements of the basic unit to which he or she belongs (elements 5 and 6). The basic unit is related operationally to the institution in terms of the specification of its budget and the institutional requirements on its curricular and/or research programmes (elements 6 and 7). Each institution in its turn is dependent on the acceptance by the central authorities of new types of course provision and, in the autonomous sector, on the allocation of funds from the total pool available for the system as a whole (elements 7 and 8). This is so even where the central authority relies on academic peer assessments to guide its decisions: the final decision nevertheless rests with the authority itself.

The vertical relationships are different in character. Where the horizontal links ensure normal day-to-day working, the vertical involve possible departures from convention. As long as the normative and operational modes are in phase with one another, the system as a whole can be said to be in dynamic equilibrium — if not in harmony, then at least in a state of balanced tension. But when the two modes become significantly out of phase, some kind of adjustment is necessary to avoid breakdown and to restore the possibility of normal functioning. On the whole, one would expect the normative level to exercise dominance over the operational. This would constitute a particular application of the general rule that, when there is a clash between what people do and what their basic values are, then the values will affect the actions more strongly than the actions affect the values. However, numerous examples of the opposite effect can be put forward: we shall examine some of them in Chapter 9.

Looking at the different relationships briefly in turn, we have noted that they are all characterized by developmental change designed to restore a sense of equilibrium. As far as the individual level is concerned (elements 1 and 5), the emphasis is on developments in working practice — for example, changes in a student's learning habits induced by changes in his or her beliefs; or changes in a researcher's emphasis and approach brought about by some new apprehension of the subject; or changes in a teacher's techniques generated by a new pedagogic ideal. The interaction between the normative and operational modes at the level of the basic unit (elements 2 and 6) will perhaps most often be characterized by developments in curricula, as group values develop in such a way as to call into question current activities — a recent example would be the effect on undergraduate courses of the changing conceptions of geography as a discipline. At the institutional level (elements 3 and 7), the characteristic product of a tension between norms and operations is some change in academic or administrative organization, designed to bring what is done more closely into line with what is held desirable. The comparable task at the level of the central authorities (elements 4 and 8) — namely, matching the provision within the system as a whole to major changes in the demands of society and the economy — often has to be tackled by a major structural reform (as in Sweden) or by the establishment of a series of new institutions (as in Britain).

The Completion of the Model

The various considerations brought forward so far can be effectively summarized by presenting them as in Figure 2.1.

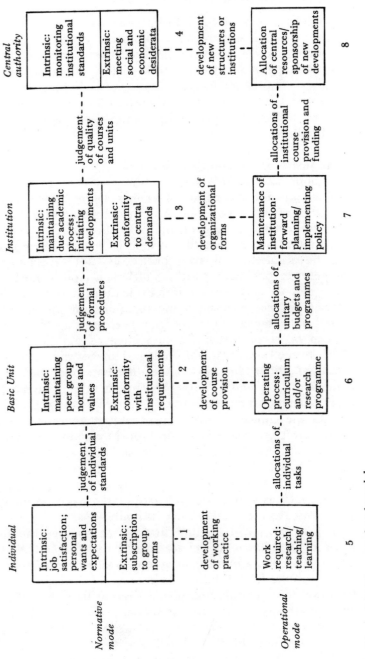

Figure 2.1 The completed model

The model which we have now set out contains no features which have not already been discussed. However, the act of bringing them together in a relatively compact form will, we hope, make it easier to keep the system as a whole in view — and hence to grasp more clearly the nature of its components and the interrelationships between them. We shall be putting this possibility to the test in the chapters which follow.

Some Justifications and Qualifications

It is important at this stage in the argument to reiterate that we are not making any sweeping claims for the model. In particular, we have no intention of implying that it is the only conceivable, or indeed the only allowable, representation of the higher education system in Britain. There could well be a number of such portrayals, not necessarily in competition one with another; different models might be concerned to emphasize different features and to develop distinct but not necessarily incompatible interpretations of shared phenomena. What we have been putting forward so far can be seen, perhaps, as a system of notation within which to spell out ideas and findings, hunches and categorical assertions about the workings of the enterprise and of its component elements, about the interactions between the parts and about their respective relationships with the whole.

That the choice of a particular kind of notation is not a purely arbitrary matter can be brought out by contrasting the Roman with the Chinese system of representing speech, or the Arabic with the Roman system of representing number. It is none the less incumbent upon anyone putting forward a schema such as ours to demonstrate that it makes reasonably good sense, and to acknowledge its limitations.

It may be asked, in the first place, whether the four levels defined in the model are generally useful. Outside the UK, admittedly, a number of systems (for example, those of Japan and the USA)[2] have nothing exactly corresponding to the level of 'central authority'. Even within the UK, its appropriateness could be questioned, since it might be argued that an additional tier is necessary in the maintained sector of polytechnics and colleges to accommodate the Regional Advisory Councils. Similarly, in some small mono-

technic institutions the level of 'basic unit' seems hardly to
exist; in some very large institutions the position is complicated by the apparent existence of sub-institutions.

Earlier in this chapter we remarked that the levels should
be seen as denoting different functions within the system,
and not as categorizing particular entities: the same individual
or corporate group might be identified at one time as performing a role at one level, and at another time, a different
role at another level. However, it seems necessary — in
addition to this particular means of giving flexibility to our
descriptive vocabulary — to introduce a further ruling to take
into account the type of objection just outlined. We shall
therefore have recourse at this point to the mathematician's
notion of a 'degenerate case' — although we shall use the
term 'special case' to avoid possible connotations of de-
bauchery or disintegration.

In so far as we might wish to extend our model to other
decentralized systems, we could say that, just as a straight
line is a special (degenerate) case of a circle — that is, a circle
with infinite radius — so too a system without any single
central authority is a special case of a system. It will usually
have a series of governing authorities (trustees for private
institutions, state administrations for public) rather than
a single and unifying one. Nevertheless, these authorities
severally will discharge the kinds of function attributed in
our model to the unitary central agency. Similarly, the
absence of basic units in small institutions can be seen as a
special case of the model, in which the second and third
levels — and the normative and operational functions of the
institution and basic unit — are combined in one entity.

If the apparent absence of a particular level is usefully
regarded as a special case of the model, the suggested addition
of further levels raises different problems about the ways in
which values, entering through the normative mode, are
expressed in institutional form. Following the principle of
Occam's razor, we should not elaborate levels beyond those
necessary for explanation. In this spirit, the Regional Advisory
Councils need not be regarded as constituting a distinct
level between the central authorities and the institutions
because, ultimately, the RACs merely make recommendations
upon which the central authorities (in this instance, the

Council for National Academic Awards and the business and technical education councils) then take decisions. Equally, the existence of federal institutions (the universities of London and Wales) does not call for an elaboration of the model, since the functions ascribed by the model to the institution are merely in these instances distributed to components of the aggregate.

To clarify this point, a distinction may be drawn between the constitutional framework of higher education — which can be depicted as a particular constellation of managerial elements arranged in formally designated organizational tiers — and the underlying structure of the system, which our model seeks to portray. The notion of organizational tiers is one which we shall need to develop in more detail when we look at other areas of social policy in Chapter 10.

While the number of tiers is a matter of administrative definition, the number of levels can be marked off in terms of significant differences in value sets. The central authority has the responsibility for collating the demands of society on the higher education system, in terms of its consumers (the employers of graduates and the potential students) and of its sponsors (the taxpaying public and its elected representatives). It has the further responsibility of seeing that the system meets such demands to an acceptable degree. The institution (as we shall later argue in Chapter 5) has its own distinctive values. Its primary task is to maintain and develop a collective character, style and reputation, incorporating but reaching beyond those of its constituent basic units; and as part of this to respond to internal and external demands by the initiation of new units and new programmes. It also has an important secondary task, of acting in its fiduciary role of collating values and monitoring the procedures of constituent units. The basic unit has the very different responsibility of responding to and maintaining academic norms within its particular field of relevance. And the values of the individual are again separable from, though comprising part of, those of the basic unit.

The distinction which is embodied in the model between the two modes, normative and operational, can also be called into question. For example, the allocation of resources within an institution can properly be seen as a value-laden activity — in other words, one which reflects judgements of merit as well as answering functional needs. But even allowing for the close interrelationships between the normative and the operational modes, there is a familiar and recognizable difference between the rationale of a group or organization and what it does in practice, between its espoused causes and its functions, its values and its tasks. The distinction is useful precisely because it separates for the purposes of analysis two quite different perspectives from which the workings of the higher education system and its constituents can be viewed. The duality is in no sense meant to imply that we are dealing with two separate systems, or two systems which are interconnected in some mysterious way: it is, as we suggested earlier, the same system, analysed from two different perspectives.

The remaining constituent of the model, namely the set of relationships between the different levels and different modes, is similarly open to qualification. Our model clearly implies that the only connecting links are those between adjacent elements. In so far as there are links between components other than those directly shown (for example, between institution and individual, leapfrogging the basic unit, in the normative mode; or diagonally between central authority in the normative mode and institution in the operational mode), we prefer to redescribe them in terms of the existing model so as to preserve its simplicity, unless this does violence to the facts. (In the examples above, we would reinterpret the leapfrogging as two horizontal moves, from institution to basic unit and basic unit to individual, with the basic unit as a dormant partner; and would redescribe the diagonal link as one vertical and one horizontal move, with the institution in its normative mode as a dummy agent.)

A further point arises which is empirical rather than conceptual: namely, what is the actual frequency, within higher education, with which diagonal, leapfrogging or other types of links are made between non-adjacent elements in the system as portrayed in our model? We suggest that the proportion of such connections is relatively low. Even in the apparently most common case, where a central authority would appear at the normative level to be directly judging the academic quality of basic units, it is not misleading to say that the institution plays some shadowy role. At the very least, its permission is formally sought for any site visitation. For the most part, we have been unable to identify clear cases of diagonal moves: the link between normative and operational modes is easily enough made at the same level in the system, but normally occurs only indirectly, it would seem, between elements at different levels. So the notation we have adopted is not only convenient in presentational terms, but also gives a fair reflection of existing practice.

An Implicit Component
The initial presentation and subsequent examination of our model has omitted one important component whose influence on higher education we shall have frequent occasion to note. We refer to the social and economic climate within which any given higher education system exists. It impinges most obviously on the central authority but also has a direct bearing on the institution, the basic unit and the individual within the system.

A society which holds higher education in considerable esteem, as do those of the USA and the Netherlands, for example, will give rise to a very different morale within academia from that generated by a society which denies its academic institutions any significance in the scheme of things (as was until recently the case in Mainland China). But more specifically, institutions whose graduates do well on the job market will tend to have more confidence than those whose record in this respect is poor; the fortunes of particular basic units will wax and wane with the extent to which their particular areas of coverage match or fail to match the prevailing social mood (consider, for instance, theology); and individual academics' self-esteem will to some extent be affected by the comparability of their salary scales with those of other professionals, including fellow-academics in other countries.

Such considerations, though extraneous to the values of higher education *per se*, undeniably influence those values, and the ways in which they are operationalized. But they are not part of the higher education system — unless one regards the whole of society as being, in a sense, the higher education system. The social and economic climate pervades higher education and acts, to change the metaphor, as a field of force affecting the development of the values which express themselves through the normative mode — and hence the operations of higher education. Thus any historical treatment of higher education would take the social and economic background as an essential context within which to explain the way in which the academic enterprise has developed.

We propose, having drawn attention to this missing component, to leave it out of the structure of our model. That is to say, we propose to confine our model to the domain of higher education, rather than extending it to embrace the wider polity. However, we do not in any way intend by this to neglect or disallow the importance, in understanding how the higher education system functions, of more general social and economic considerations. What we have here designated as the background to our model will be a recurring feature of our subsequent discussion.

3. The Development of Higher Education: Changing Purposes Since 1945

History and our Model

In this chapter, we look mainly at some developments in British universities in order to show how our model can be illustrated by historical evidence. The theme is that of the central authorities — particularly the University Grants Committee — and their relationships over time to the universities and to the wider political and social environment. We shall try to establish how the history of higher education, and particularly that of the universities in the UK since 1945, substantiates our claims that the central authorities mediate social and economic expectations through their allocative decisions, and that other levels in the model respond to pressures from the external environment.

A central part of our argument will be that the social expectations of expansion, and the consequences of it, were internalized to become the accepted norms of most institutions and basic units.[1] These shifts of attitude first gave rise to large-scale increases in student numbers to accommodate the broadened purposes of higher education as well as the pressures of changing demography. The new purposes themselves were, however, then modified by the alterations in the size and nature of the student clientele.

These quantitative and qualitative changes in their turn led to two major adjustments to the system as a whole. First, the virtual monopoly of the universities was broken by the creation of the binary system. This was itself the most important indicator of the second change — the strengthening role of the state. The hegemony of the central authorities over large areas of newly restructured advanced education increased steadily, as did their bargaining power with the universities. From these two consequences flowed changes in the UGC and the creation of new intermediaries such as the Council for National Academic Awards (CNAA) which took up a powerful role in relation to the public sector institutions.

Thus changing values in the larger environment affected the beliefs and actions of the central authorities. Yet structural relationships continued largely unchanged: we would argue that this was because norm-setting in the basic unit still remained a dominant feature of the system. Higher education continues to survive by accommodating the tensions between potentially conflicting elements. These tensions, which are intrinsic to the nature of the enterprise, were remarked over a long period, and without disapproval, by the UGC[2] in their published reports.

Our model allows for two antinomies implicit in the governance of British higher education. The first is that while the freedom of the basic unit is a dominant academic norm, the central authorities influence the higher education system so as to make its norms compatible with the needs of the society which nourishes and sanctions it. The second contradiction is that although higher education has changed in response to the social expectations authoritatively placed by government and others on it, it has also persistently demonstrated a contra-functionalism, a different view of society and its needs, embodied in the obstinacies of the academic way of life. It nurtures beliefs that the growth and transmission of knowledge are legitimate in themselves, not depending for their right to flourish on stated public demands; and that it is a proper function of academic institutions to act as centres of alternative opinions within the political system.

This second contradiction persists in higher education in all of its forms, now as in the past.[3] It is evidence of society's need (or higher education's ability to convince society of its need) to nourish criticism from the same sources as it sustains for its supply of skilled manpower and leadership. Higher education is not alone in embodying such a contradiction. The judiciary, for example, are both 'lions under the throne' — in Francis Bacon's phrase — and testers and critics of the way in which public authorities implement the law.

Academic Norms Under Pressure from Expansion

The 1939—45 War was the starting point for changes which eventually became codified and promulgated in the 1960s. Some of the University Grants Committee's statements in the early postwar years reflect the changes that took place:

> there was an artificial extension of university activities . . . directly related to the various and developing needs of the war machine . . . there has emerged from the war a new and sustained public interest in the universities and a strong realization of the unique contribution they had to offer to the national wellbeing, whether in peace or war. Any conception that may have existed of the universities as places of cultural luxury catering for a small and privileged class has faded away and will not return. A heightened sense of social justice generated by the war has opened the door more widely than ever before . . .[4]

At this time, it might be noted, the competent authorities were promoting the 'opportunity', or the 'soft', concept of equality which sought to ensure that the able, from whatever social class, would find their way to university and thence to the heights of the social system.

The UGC's last report before the war (1936) had looked forward to a period in which 'quantitative growth would be less rapid than hitherto and it will be possible for the universities to concentrate their attention on questions of quality'. In 1948, too, 'the dominating task which confronts the universities is that of maintaining, and ultimately of improving, the quality of university education notwithstanding a pressure in student numbers hitherto unknown'.[5] The UGC and the universities were thus driven on by three potentially conflicting motives. First, society needed educated manpower: compared with other countries, Britain's output of graduates was disconcertingly low. Second, the equality of sacrifice in the war should lead to a much greater measure of social and educational equality than existed before the war. Third, academic balance and quality must be retained.

On the first of these points, the Barlow Committee (1946)[6] proposed a doubling of output of scientists and technologists. It argued for an increase of the university system from 50 000 to 90 000 as soon as possible. It is a mistake to assume that all was stagnant before the 1960s. Two years after the Barlow recommendation, in 1948/9, there were already 83 000 students. The increases were mainly to be found in the provincial universities although, for example, Oxford had increased its overall numbers by 50 per cent over the prewar total.

In specifying the changes in scale necessary to meet the new social and economic objectives, the central authorities did not avoid setting academic norms, though the UGC would always claim to indicate rather than prescribe. In the early postwar years, the aim was to ensure a good spread of disciplines so that there was contact between students in different fields.[7] The UGC therefore resisted the notion of technological universities for a long time. It was concerned about quality and shared the views of the Barlow Committee that 'in few other fields are numbers of so little value compared to quality properly developed . . . Moreover, before [a student] enters the university, intelligence must be trained and the associated personal qualities matured to a standard that we would not wish to see lowered.'[8]

Joining the debate, the Committee of Vice-Chancellors and Principals, in a note on university planning and finance for the decade 1947–56, warned that 'academic standards once lowered are not retrievable, and Gresham's law applies to them'. The Barlow Committee had, however, thought that 'on the evidence of certain intelligence tests there is an ample reserve of intelligence to allow university numbers to be doubled and standards to be raised concurrently'. The UGC's own view was that 'no reliable conclusions concerning the future supply of students of a probable quality can be drawn from the present situation'.

In any event, the new Education Act would increase the numbers of pupils in full-time education until 18 and thus increase the supply of potential undergraduates. Not only would ability be tested, but also 'character, temperament and wider qualities of mind'. The UGC duly endorsed the egalitarian impulses to which the war gave rise: 'It is clearly desirable to exclude one type of student whom the possession of means once entitled to secure admittance; that is the riotously living pass-man, sometimes of athletic promise, on whom the university as an agency of culture made small dint.'

These statements are clearly indicative of the ways in which the central authorities — here the UGC — accommodated to social and economic demands. The institutions in their turn responded, and at a cost. The standards of life in the universities deteriorated with the increased numbers. The UGC was rightly anxious lest the quality of staff, their teaching ratios, the buildings and the provision of office accommodation should deteriorate, and the improvement in quality to which it had looked forward in its last prewar report would be further postponed. Before the war, for example, the staffing ratio at Oxbridge had improved from 1:11 in 1934/5 to 1:10 in 1938/9, and similar improvements took place elsewhere in many universities in the early post-war period. There were, however, no rooms for discussion groups or individual tuition and there were long queues in the refectories. The life of a professor was not one of gilded charm. In one place, as many as four professors occupied one not very large office. Junior staff might be four to six — or even, in one university, nine — to a room. Ratios improved again in the 1950s.

The UGC report for 1935–47 anticipated the time, twenty years hence, when the expanding numbers of staff in the universities would produce major problems. In fact promotion blockages never occurred at that time because of further expansion of the universities. The UGC also deplored the heavy demands of administration placed on professors and heads of departments. As a result, research was in danger of being undertaken only by junior staff. There were too many calls to serve on committees outside the universities. The increased load on non-professorial staff was perhaps one of the reasons why universities were asked to keep such staff informed of current academic and financial issues and to foster in them, by whatever means possible, a sense of administrative responsibility. At this stage, however, there was no hint that junior academics had any part to play in the government of their universities.

The central authorities were understandably concerned with more than the increase in numbers. For example, the UGC deplored postgraduate studies that reflected only the 'specific endowment of research', or 'narrowly specialized fields of enquiry not all of which have particular educational value', or 'over-emphasis on original work, however trivial'. Interestingly, it took the view that 'the risk of absorption in sterile forms of so-called research is greater in the arts than in science and technology'.

The UGC was in effect operating on two conflicting premisses. It had views about matters of academic substance, but was always concerned that the institutions and basic units should make the running: it was for them to propose while the UGC disposed. Yet the UGC's reading of social needs and of desirable academic developments, including the maintenance of particular academic norms and styles, led it to make operational decisions about which institutions or basic units to support. All institutions were excellent but some were more excellent than others. Moreover, from 1945 onwards the UGC was required to identify developments that should be promoted: its backing, in terms of specially earmarked funds, was crucial for the development of social sciences after the war.

In using its power, the UGC developed pragmatic principles from which to work. The criterion of need meant that the small and financially weak institutions received a higher proportion of grant than their student numbers would otherwise justify. This principle, however, was qualified. Writing in 1948, the UGC stated that its intention had been to help those who were able to find money for themselves, to support quality and thus direct money where it seemed most likely to produce the best results. 'We did not regard it as a proper object of policy to use our financial influence in such a way as to obliterate existing variations of academic prestige.'[9] Thus, the norms to be endorsed were not only that of national need but also that of intellectual quality as perceived by the institutions themselves, their peers who judged them and their benefactors who might be attracted to excellence. The UGC articulated the values of academe and acted on them.

Growth and Norm-Setting

The academic principle of excellence and elitism was, however, in tension with the social need for rapid growth. In the first postwar period of expansion, the smaller universities and colleges took a large part of the increase in student population. Thus numbers influenced a pattern hitherto based on prestige. Inevitably this reduced the rewards that a sympathetic state gave to those who pursued excellence, although the UGC moved only reluctantly from the earlier criterion. It did not much want to equalize professorial salaries, and

in this as in other things 'it seemed to some of us questionable whether government funds should be used for the
purpose of depriving certain universities of advantages which
they had built up over a long period'.[10] But other considerations pointed towards an opposite conclusion. Unless the
weaker universities and colleges were enabled to offer salaries
more nearly comparable to those prevailing elsewhere, they
would obviously find difficulty in attracting to their chairs
more than a very small proportion of men and women of
first-class attainment.

In the years following the immediate postwar period
(1947—52) there was a hiccough in growth. The UGC thought
that the student population might have reached a peak. It
also hoped that when the upward movement was resumed
the increase might be gradual.[11] Thus there would be a
period in which to consolidate, develop and experiment. The
essential functions of universities would continue to be
those of doing original work, of creating knowledge, and of
producing the next generation of scholars and leaders. Such
developments as were contemplated were educational rather
than social: students should have a broader education. The
UGC sustained the liberal and humanistic view of an elite
system. It did not take up or advocate, for example, closer
relationships between universities and their immediate
communities, or emphasize the vocational aspects of education.

At that time, with numbers much increased (science and
technology doubling, and arts subjects growing by 68 per
cent between 1938 and 1952) the UGC began to wrestle with
the difficulties of estimating employment demands. There
were now one in thirty-one of the relevant age-group, compared with one in sixty before the war, entering university
in Great Britain: should the proportion grow further? The
UGC noted that the Committee on Scientific Manpower had
not thought it wise to aim at raising the university student
population in the country to the American scale 'at the cost
of so great a decline in entrance standards'. The UGC would
welcome an increase, but subject to three conditions. First, it
would want to ensure that there would be satisfactory
employment for graduates. Second, accommodation and
equipment should be adequate. Third, there should be no

decline in standards. At the beginning of 1953 the UGC argued that the proportions both of the really good and of the really poor students were lower. There were many more second-class candidates. There could not be great increases in numbers without reducing quality.[12]

The Committee's associated concern with academic independence was reflected in indirect ways. In particular, money reaching universities from government rather than from private benefactors or the UGC was thought of as tainted. There might be no immediate danger from taking on a larger number of government contracts, but only because most government research took place outside the universities. It should not, however, be overdone. Again, the UGC was reluctant to earmark funds for particular developments. The universities should determine their own excellences and not be over-responsive to central influence. We might look forward here to the movement of norms in these areas of policy. There is less anxiety nowadays about earmarking. The universities are much more explicitly dependent on central funding and expect to respond to central indications of social need. Contract research may still be viewed with suspicion but is known to be a way to extend the range of activities, and to gain more staffing, in hard times. 'Soft money' can become 'hard' if good research is thought worthy of permanent sponsoring by a research council or the UGC or, on rolling contract, by a government department.

In the 1950s the universities and the emergent institutions within the public sector increasingly came under public view, partly because of the political ascendancy of those, such as David Eccles, who believed in an opportunity state, directly related to economic growth. Industry began to recruit many more graduate trainees, and the university began to figure more prominently as a means to employment in the minds of students than as membership of a civilizing community.

At the same time, the universities experienced the problems created by increased dependency on the state, which caused the UGC itself to become party to a more *dirigiste* attitude at the centre. As the system grew, so did somewhat more systematic policy-making. University salaries were made uniform. Because in the 1960s five institutions received charters within five years, the UGC was compelled to take, and to express, a view of what universities should be like. For example, in deciding to encourage the creation of a university college at Sussex, it took account of where it should be located and of the optimum size and range of courses it should offer. Some demands for universities to be established elsewhere were turned down. The process of vetting such bids inevitably caused the UGC to build up criteria.

The assertion of stronger central policy was a direct consequence of growth. More A level passes in the schools meant greater pressure for places. Yet university standards were rising, as measured by such indicators as the increasing number of students able to be accommodated in places away from home and the improvement in staffing ratios from 1:10·2 in 1939 to 1:8·6 in 1952, and then to 1:7·2 in 1957. The resulting increases in cost led inevitably to the need for control.[13]

With all of this, the norm of university autonomy remained strong. The UGC deprecated any attempt to regard research as an activity separate from teaching, 'partly because it might give the impression that useful guidance could be given from the centre on the balance of effort between teaching and research'.[14] It hoped that the universities would continue to ensure that the acceptance of outside support was consistent with the balanced development of their work. (Only some twenty years later, government demands for relevant research were made manifest not only through the UGC but even through the research councils,[15] the main sources of independent academic finance in Britain.)

The UGC still remained resistant to new forms of higher education. As we have noted, it did not at first embrace willingly the notion of the technological university. 'We should regard the isolation of the institutions confined to a narrow range of subjects as unfavourable to high attainment.' So it pressed forward instead with the expansion of Imperial College, London.

Throughout this period the UGC was able to promote expansion while maintaining the classic relationship between state and universities, in which the UGC was regarded by the universities as the guardian of their liberties — the buffer between government and universities as one UGC chairman put it[16] — and by government as responsible for seeing that increasing sums from the public purse were spent to the best advantage in the national interest. Thus the technique of control from the centre was that of negotiation rather than that of managerial diktat. These characteristics still persist.

The UGC report for 1961 remarked on three distinct phases of development which could be identified since 1946.[17] Until 1953 the UGC refurbished the universities for those whose education had been interrupted. If it was not to be business as usual, higher education was certainly not to spring too far out of the classic mould, even though newly available to a larger proportion of the population. Between 1952 and 1962 there was 'the trend' of voluntary staying-on at school, which brought pressure from qualified entrants for expansion. And now the UGC noted how the trend was being overtaken by the 'bulge' caused by the increase in birth rate immediately after the war. Already a university population of 200 000 was being contemplated. The UGC cautiously wondered whether the economy would be able to take the strain of these increases and whether particular subject needs might not be too strongly asserted against balanced development. It began, too, 'to pay close attention to developments elsewhere in the national structure of higher education'.[18]

Expansion and the Binary Principle

The Robbins Report, as the UGC remarked,[19] did not institute expansion in the universities or in the public sector institutions. At the end of 1967, well before the Robbins Report had worked its way through the system, there were already 184 000 students and nearly 24 000 academic staff in the universities. The report instead established, publicly and authoritatively, the principles of development for higher education in this country. The Robbins Committee was itself an example of how central authorities develop policy by co-opting both those who speak to societal needs and those who respond to professional norms. The chairman was a leading academic but government assessors were deeply involved. So, too, were other academics and representatives of local government and the schools. Among other things, the report created the case for the conferment of degrees by bodies other than universities: and the universities were compelled to consider their plans in relationship to those of other institutions.

Anthony Crosland's Woolwich speech, made on 27 April 1965, set the seal on this policy.

> On the one hand we have what has come to be called the autono-
> mous sector, represented by the universities, in whose ranks, of
> course, I now include the colleges of advanced technology. On the
> other hand we have the public sector, represented by the leading
> technical colleges and the colleges of education. The Government
> accepts this dual system as being fundamentally the right one,
> with each sector making its own distinctive contribution to the
> whole. We infinitely prefer it to the alternative concept of a unitary
> system, hierarchically arranged on the 'ladder' principle, with the
> universities at the top and the other institutions down below.

The UGC fully endorsed the binary system and in so doing accepted what some would regard as artificial differentiations. The universities were to be more national than local in their recruitment, more free to determine their own field of academic activity and standards, and had their freedoms safeguarded by an independent University Grants Committee. The non-university sector would teach undergraduate courses in conjunction with non-degree work and would thus be 'vertically comprehensive'. It would be regionally or locally oriented, largely controlled and directly financed by public authorities. It would meet national needs but also the require-ments of local industry and other forms of local demand.

These proposals were finally endorsed in the White Paper of May 1965, *A Plan for Polytechnics and Other Colleges*.[20] At this point, the UGC became apprehensive as it saw how large would be the increase in the number of full-time degree courses to be provided within the public sector. (The appre-hensions were to be fully justified. Government has done much to bring polytechnics into parity with the universities. Staff salaries[21] and student numbers are decided, if not equally, then with reference to the potential of both sectors.) The pressures on the universities from the competing sector developed at the very time when the demand for higher education became uncertain and the money available to nourish it more difficult to guarantee.

The creation of the binary system can be viewed as a dramatic intervention in both the norms and operations of higher education, and as an affirmation that public purposes should be determined outside higher education proper. It can also be seen as a governmental assertion of the antinomy, discussed at the beginning of this chapter, between academic independence and conformity to social demands.

The universities themselves had diverse origins. Some were set up on the initiative of groups of scholars, and others on the initiative of civic or private or ecclesiastical authorities. In contrast, 'the technical colleges were more the children of towns, or rather of town councils, administrative bodies which wanted to administer the new institutions, to press them and keep them in the mould which they saw as most appropriate to the demands of the city'.[22] Hence their service tradition and Crosland's attempt to establish a separate sector for a different purpose, but one of equal merit. The polytechnics derived in part from an attempt to achieve equal educational opportunity for all, including those candidates of merit who did not find it easy to come in through the traditional route to the universities. The non-university institutions were intended, too, to provide for innovation in the field of higher education in ways of which the universities were felt to be incapable. They represented a subtle form of pressure by the government. The government would not and could not instruct the universities to change their ways. Instead, it set up an alternative system to bring about by other means what was thought to be necessary in the public interest. The polytechnics must fit their advanced courses into regional plans, and submit to a measure of local authority control and DES building programmes, and so be more firmly planned than the universities could be.

The case of the polytechnics demonstrates, however, that the basic characteristics of higher education cannot easily be overridden. The polytechnics steadily moved towards the modes and aspirations of the universities in what Burgess and Pratt have called 'academic drift'.[23] The universities in their turn moved towards adaptations of their course offerings designed to meet identifiable market needs. The distinctions between the two types of institution had within a decade become embarrassingly blurred, and the system, in the perception of staff, students and employers, came to resemble increasingly the 'ladder' which Crosland had deplored.

The Council for National Academic Awards, founded in 1964 to regulate standards for degrees awarded outside universities, has adopted norms not far different from those that any senate would apply to the behaviour of basic units. It has demanded comparable academic standards in all advanced higher education institutions, through its visitations and its panels which approve courses, as well as through its insistence on the use of external examiners. It urges minimum standards of resource provision as well as of academic freedom for the polytechnics and their departments. In effect, it has adopted university traditions, practices and criteria, as the Robbins Committee intended it should. Although it acted throughout its first decade as 'a relatively passive institution, more content to be the recipient of external pressure than the active initiator of policy',[24] its role became more assertive towards the end of the 1960s. More recently it has argued that comparability with university standards requires sustained support and encouragement for research in the polytechnics. It has considered the DES not to be obviously apprised of this need.

The Changing Norms
As the polytechnics developed and the Robbins planning figures were first achieved and then overtaken, the principles of higher education began to shift. The Robbins principle of open access to all who were qualified greatly altered the scope and ethos of higher education. And the assertion of the public ethic, of meeting the needs of society through more economically and socially relevant studies, is more significant to our purpose, as a critique of traditional institutions, than is the success the polytechnics have actually achieved. These have been proclaimed as the specialty of the polytechnics although all of the postwar UGC reports give evidence of such movements, over a long time, in universities.

At the same time, the changes in client groups and the reciprocal weakening of authority in traditional institutions affected the whole academic milieu. Thus, if higher education traditionally was private, elite and eclectic in its purposes (and such was the caricature of its pre-expansion nature) it had certainly become far more open and socially responsive at the end of the period of expansion. Even before the economic blizzards of the early 1970s set in, academia seemed ready to acknowledge the need to respond to society's demands — always on the understanding that it would do so in its own ways, rather than those perceived by the central authorities, whose monopoly of understanding on these matters universities persistently questioned.

Changes in Central Authorities

The power of government has grown in recent years: but that is no new phenomenon. Government intervention has always been possible,[25] if more often concerned with the constitutional arrangements than with the purposes of higher education. There were perceptible interventions by governments through the succession of Royal Commissions in the nineteenth and twentieth centuries which strongly affected the development of the Scottish universities (1826), the universities of Oxford and Cambridge (1850), the University of London (1909) and the University of Wales (1916). There had been a Privy Council 'trial' in 1902 to determine whether the Victoria University should be divided into separate autonomous universities in Lancashire and Yorkshire.[26] Controversies over the relationship between St Andrews University and Dundee University College led to a special UGC visitation in 1951 and a subsequent Royal Commission to settle the matter.[27]

More than this, the establishment has never shied away from redefining the purposes of higher education. In the early years of the present century Haldane and others argued for a connected system of education in universities, schools and colleges, to be organized in regions, each with a university as a 'brain and intelligence' of the whole, with teacher training as part of the university function. It was proposed that the organization should be decentralized and that the pattern of curricula should both provide culture and apply scientific and other forms of knowledge to practical life. Haldane was more interventionist than most, but this duality had been preached by Matthew Arnold thirty years before and was later to be advocated by Lyon Playfair, T. H. Huxley and Henry Roscoe. (In contrast Lord Davey, chairman of the commission making statutes for the University of London in 1898, doubted 'whether the two objects — culture and professional training — can be carried on concurrently in a university'.)[28] Thus even in Britain, where university autonomy has persisted most strongly, there has never been a concept of academic freedom that has eschewed connections with practical problems or professional training.

From the beginning of the postwar period, the UGC had no illusions about the implications of increased government support. Hitherto the sums given to the universities were small even if they were on the increase. Grants were intended, as the UGC itself noted,[29] not to stimulate active policies of expansion and development but to encourage and facilitate improvements which the universities could make within a relatively stable financial framework. Government grants did not dictate the pace of progress. Between the two wars state interference and control were at a minimum. In 1938 grants were about one-third of the universities' total revenue. But by 1946 the Committee of Vice-Chancellors (in a note on university policy and finance) was able to assert that

> Universities entirely accept the view that the government has not only the right, but the duty to satisfy itself that every field of study which in the national interest ought to be cultivated in Great Britain is in fact being cultivated in the university system and that the resources which are placed at the disposal of universities are being used with full regard both to efficiency and economy.

In the event, the UGC chose to perform these functions on behalf of government, not by direction but by stimulation, co-ordination and advice.

The most important evidence of the negotiative style was the maintenance of the quinquennial grant system. Universities received a block grant for recurrent expenses (capital grants were negotiated separately) to last for a five-year period. Supplementation for unavoidable increases in such costs as university salaries could, however, be allowed. The quinquennial system released both institutions and central authorities from detailed annual control and enabled the universities to pursue their own ends, once agreed in broad outline with the UGC, over a reasonably long planning period.

The UGC's decisions nevertheless answered to changes in the style and purpose of the central authorities as a whole.

The second half of the 1960s was the period of manpower planning, of the ill-fated National Plan,[30] of optimism about the capability of planners to predict needs and specify institutions which would meet them. The Committee did not itself feel able to translate general expressions of need into particular numbers and types of output. For guidance on national and manpower requirements, it looked to the government through the Department of Education and Science — although it thought, realistically enough, that because demand could not be predicted, flexibility in the training of university graduates was necessary.

The UGC believed, as did the Robbins Committee, that entry to university courses was something over which universities had no direct control and that the size and balance of the flow of candidates to admission could not be closely related to national needs for graduate manpower. In this connection, one of the Robbins principles, which became government policy, was all-important: 'Courses of higher education should be available for all those who are qualified by ability and attainment to pursue them and who wish to do so.'

In its postwar reports, the UGC frequently referred to its role *vis-à-vis* the universities and government. The Committee thought it essential that it should be able to make a regular review in depth of university needs and university efficiency, both collectively and between one university and another.[31] It stood firm on the quinquennial freedoms, as well as on the principle of its being a buffer or shock-absorber between government and the universities. Anthony Crosland did not controvert this principle when he decided in 1967 that the universities should be open to audit; but the buffer function of the Committee inevitably changed with the changes in the university system's scope and size. The increase of university institutions from twenty-four in 1944 to forty-three in 1967 made it all the more necessary that the Committee should exercise a positive role. It also had to consider what provision was being offered in non-university institutions. The universities began to see themselves as only a part, 'if a distinguished part', of the nation's provision for higher education. The creation of the technological universities had already widened both the popular and the professional notions of what universities were for. On top of all this, the UGC saw the need to take cognizance of what the research councils might do.

These developments caused inevitable changes in the structural position of the UGC and its relation to government. At first, there seemed to be no significant implication in the transfer of central government responsibility for universities from the Treasury to the DES, which followed a minority report of the Robbins Committee. It meant that university education could be related to developments elsewhere, and DES ministers could argue with the Treasury, which lost the embarrassment of being a spending department negotiating with itself about allocations. It was only later that a more directive style began to be adopted. This is commonly thought to have occurred with the allocations announced in 1967, when UGC preferences on the balance between different subjects and between the numbers of undergraduates and postgraduates were first stated in detail. It is anybody's guess whether the quinquennial arrangements would have survived, even in the absence of the financial retrenchment, accompanied by a reduction in student demand, which precipitated a new system of short-term budgeting for universities in the early 1970s.

In 1976 the UGC had to report a conclusive downturn in the process of growth and a series of *ad hoc* decisions related to changing national pressures: 'As a result there is a deep and damaging sense of uncertainty which can only be removed by the restoration of the longer term planning horizons.' It was accepted that the taxpayers should receive full value for money. By the early 1970s, the UGC was already exerting influence on universities to specialize and concentrate their offerings. This led to adjustments in the number of places in particular subjects such as agriculture and forestry, area studies, mining, metallurgy and agricultural economics, although such measures were not unknown before. The UGC had also begun to take account of developments on the other side of the binary line which were brought into its deliberations through discussion with the DES.[32] But it continued strongly to defend the principle of university autonomy, which was not only a recognition of academic freedom but also, it maintained, exemplified good management practice.

Norms and Operations

How do these accounts of changes in the central authorities' relations with the universities throw light on our model? Our argument has illustrated how the norms and operations of the central authorities can impinge upon individual institutions. As the purposes of higher education began to widen, largely under the impress of such external forces as demography, and economic and social expectation, so the sentiments of the central authorities changed. The norm of peer control of academic content remained strong, but came into increased tension with the central authorities' assumptions about how the universities should respond to social demand. Large-scale expansion of numbers, the endorsement of institutions' plans for new types of courses and new groupings of subjects, the concept of a division between private concerns and public purposes, as assumed, if never fully implemented, by the binary system — all of these were major movements of thought on the part of the central authorities. Such changes of concept were in due course translated into the operational mode, into the regulatory system, into decisions on allocations. They affected the intensity of control and the normative indications from the centre of the reasons why money was granted.

This historical dimension to the model shows how the universities, who for so long were able to regard their position in society, and indeed their means of livelihood, as a freehold — a term still used of fellowships at Oxford and Cambridge — have now come to acknowledge themselves as part of a system conditioned by market forces. Student demand is eagerly built up and identified, as witness the advertisements for courses in the serious weekly journals and newspapers.[33] The fact that higher education institutions feel themselves to be at the mercy of the market strengthens the hand of the central authorities, not only in making decisions on resources but in negotiating such changes in attitude as they consider necessary if higher education is to respond to the national need.

The central authorities and the institutions exist within changing political environments which clearly affect the content of the normative mode. To these and other parts of the system we now turn for more detailed examination.

4. Planning and Decision-Making for the Whole System

The Central Authorities and the Model
In this chapter we outline the centralized functions of British higher education and consider the ways in which central authorities work with other levels. We also discuss whether academic institutions are part of a structure that behaves systemically, in the sense that it manages to achieve compatibility at each of its levels between objectives, processes and products. This brings us into the broader questions surrounding the concept of planning as national authorities move from what is known as first-generation to second-generation planning.

The model set out in Chapter 2 includes the components and relationships illustrated in Figure 4.1. The central authorities are portrayed as maintaining certain norms which are conditioned by contemporary social and economic desiderata, and which take the form of general judgements about requisite institutional standards. These in their turn condition the specific judgements about the quality of individual institutions, courses and units, which the central authorities render operational through allocations and approvals. Decisions about which institutions to expand and which courses to maintain and develop, although allocative in their consequences, are themselves held to be a reflection of normative judgements. Chapter 3 has already provided us with examples of how these processes were set into action between 1945 and 1977. Again, however, we draw attention to the somewhat uneasy division between the central and local authority tiers (see pages 21-2) of the control over the public sector institutions.

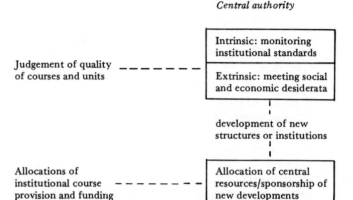

Figure 4.1   Functions of the central authorities

Central Authorities on their Own

The normative content of decision-making by the central authorities is rarely explicit. Certain general objectives can be assumed at any time, although the emphasis on each of them will vary according to context. Government in the UK is traditionally wary of proclaiming the values to which it responds in its maintenance of the higher education system. However, we may infer that it accepted, and continues to accept, the statement of objectives for higher education enunciated in the Robbins Committee report on higher education,[1] since it adopted its substantive proposals. The four main objectives can be summarized as: instruction in skills suitable to play a part in the general division of labour; the promotion of powers of the mind; the advancement of learning; and the transmission of a common culture and common standards of citizenship.

The Robbins objectives collectively provide for higher education to benefit the economy, to strengthen society in its control and cultural transmission functions, and to help the individual student seeking both personal satisfaction and qualification for employment. The emphasis laid on these four objectives has certainly changed over time. For example, the connection between higher education and economic development is now much more open to doubt than it was in the 1960s and, as a result of this, as well as of changing demography, the central authorities have ceased to assume that higher education must continue inexorably to expand. The advancement of learning is no longer considered to be a social good sufficiently overriding for resources to be given to it unhesitatingly. Higher education is now so diffuse in its functions and purposes that it is not expected automatically to transmit a common culture and common standards of citizenship: indeed, it is sometimes accused of promoting dissent rather than consensus. Different political ascendancies expect different things of higher education. The degree of support it is given varies according to what is demanded of it, and reflects the confidence that the polity has at any given time in the ability of higher education to meet social needs.

Despite the sharp and decisive fluctuations of policy that can be, and have been, induced by changes in political control, the central authorities seek to defend certain basic norms. In common with the institutions, they have the fiduciary role of preserving the continuities of relationships between the centre, its dependent agencies and the institutions they sponsor. Government is reckoned to be predictable, accountable and equitable, and to respond to social change. In theory at least, the claims of all interest groups and the merits of all proposals for change are weighed in the balance before any decisive move is made.

Inputs to the Central Authorities

The centre responds to different inputs which change over time[2] and which constitute the environment within which the normative mode is formed and modulated. Chapter 3 described many of the changes which bore the impress of movements in society, the economy and the political system over the postwar generation.

Such responses have included the transition from an elite towards a mass system; the development of more contract research in the universities; and the growth of a wider range of institutions, some of university status and others of comparable status but in the public sector. At the level of the institutions themselves, we may note the acceptance of different subject priorities, such as the growing popularity of law, and the reiterative resurgence of different forms of technology — changes which were reflected in the operational decisions of central authorities — and the demands for participation by students and junior staff within the universities, which entered charter arrangements sanctioned by the authorities, or the equivalent articles for public sector institutions. Some of the movements developed from within government itself. Others came from interests co-opted by the central authorities. Others again derived from pressure groups with connections in the wider environment. Most came from combinations of all three.

The central authorities are themselves part of a larger governmental machine which constrains or supports development as a component of policies only partly concerned with education as such. The Treasury regards higher education as an element of public sector expenditure to be allowed or disallowed growth in accordance with the country's economic policies. Other government departments have a direct interest in the ways in which higher education produces doctors, social workers, teachers or engineers, and these predictions are put directly into the central authorities' calculations of what subjects should be supported and in which basic units.

Alongside central government there are advisory bodies whose position is equivocal in the British system. We noted in Chapter 3 that there had been in the past a series of Royal Commissions which concerned themselves with the status and working constitutions of individual universities. The Percy Committee (1945)[3] pointed the way forward for the autonomy and status of technological education, culminating in the creation of ten technological universities. The Barlow Report (1946) and the Robbins Report (1963) in their turn exemplified the ways in which government reaches outside itself into an established academic and social elite. It does so primarily as a means to develop, to confirm, but also to concede to, those changing norms within the larger society which need a wider social imprimatur before their adoption as policies to be promulgated through the normative and operational modes.

In the wider context, the arguments for growth were forged by an amalgam of academic liberal advocacy and sociological research on the consequences of restricting access to higher education. There were, too, demands from schools that pressure on the upper end of secondary schooling should be relieved by the creation of more undergraduate places. And beyond them, there was a general climate of opinion in society at large in favour of academic expansion. Britain, along with other countries enjoying the economic booms of the 1950s and early 1960s, regarded education not only as an economic necessity but also as a major consumer good which ought to be distributed as part of the developing opportunity state.

In considering how central policy is formed, account also has to be taken of a whole series of pressure groups which vary in legitimacy and power. The heads of institutions are represented, in Britain, through the Committee of Vice-Chancellors and Principals and the Committee of Directors of Polytechnics. In common with the teachers' associations and unions of students, they have a dual role. They are vigilant on particular sectional issues such as the sharing-out of resources, pay or grants, and other questions affecting status and conditions. But they may also respond to (even if they seldom initiate) the main substantive issues which emerge through the policy system — although they always have problems in creating a single opinion from the multiple view of their constituents.[4]

Centrally-initiated changes are not, on the whole, the product of conflict. Central government officials may themselves expound 'academic' points of view and academics may invite intervention. Manpower planning, for example, was the product of science policies largely created on the advice of academic scientists.

The student body is the easiest to identify as a pressure group which has itself affected outcomes. Student pressures on such issues as participation, appeals procedures, and even to some extent the funding of higher education, have been formidable. They have in a variety of ways affected the ethos and the relative status systems of higher education. The change in climate has in its turn affected the way in which the central authorities have reacted. In contrast, the teachers in higher education (in common with their counterparts in other sectors) have relatively little industrial power. Their claims, weakened by the vagaries of economic and demographic performance since the expansion of the 1960s, have

become marginal to the concerns of the central authorities —
who are increasingly preoccupied with maintaining the
system within the economic disciplines asserted by the
Treasury.

However, to argue that academic pressure groups have had
little direct influence on government is not to say that academic opinion plays a negligible role in policy-making. It is
an essential feature of the advisory committee system that it
co-opts influential academics to its membership. This device
enables the government to test out in advance those policy
changes to which it is already partly disposed. Such was
certainly the case in the appointment of the Robbins Committee, as witness the instant adoption of its main recommendations. A similar mechanism drives the vehicle through
which government makes its allocations to universities. The
University Grants Committee negotiates on the major allocative decisions, on what proportion of higher education funding
shall be placed in universities; but then its largely academic
membership is expected to make judgements about how the
consequent detailed allocations shall be made. The dual role
of advocate and adjudicator requires the UGC to monitor
universities so that it can form inputs about their present
functions and future potential: and those judgements can
themselves become inputs to the government itself as it
makes its global allocations.

The Division of Tasks Between Government and the Central Authorities

The functions implied in the normative mode of the central
authorities are evaluative and judgemental; those in the
operational mode are concerned with allocating resources
and sanctioning new developments. In some systems of higher
education, both sets of functions are to be found in one
agency of government — although there can hardly be a
system which does not co-opt academics into the making of
judgements about academic quality and academic requirements.[5] In the UK, however, a clear distinction is made
between what the legislature and the executive — Westminster
and Whitehall — decide through their own machinery, and
those decisions which are delegated to the central authorities
within the higher education system who occupy a position

intermediate between government and the individual institution. Yet a further complication is the role undertaken
by the local authorities in the public sector of higher education.

The central government decides the level of resources
which will meet what it considers to be social and economic
needs; it also decides how many places shall be financed in
the different sectors of higher education, what resources to
provide for each and therefore the quality of provision.
Within the public sector it goes further, and distributes new
places to individual polytechnics and colleges and lays down
norms of staffing ratios. However, in deciding which public
institutions should receive what, government depends, to
some extent, on the advice of the Regional Advisory Councils for further education, because it approves advanced
courses jointly with the RACs.

The public sector is the subject of a particular set of
relationships which should be briefly explored here. The
arrangements depend on two linked assumptions which affect
structure. The first is that development in the public sector
should be overtly responsive to public purpose, moulded
both by national and by local or regional needs. The second
assumption is that local authorities are the appropriate
mechanism through which local needs can be articulated
and allocations made. There are thus, for the public sector,
two tiers of control beyond the institutions, which imply
two groups of social and economic criteria leading to a
double set of allocative decisions. The recurrent doubts
about the binary system and the persistent uncertainty about
local authority control of public sector higher education are
symptomatic of uncertainty about the need for, or appropriateness of, the two tiers.

In the university sector the specific financial allocations
to institutions (which carry implications for staffing ratios
and student numbers and buildings) are made on behalf of
the government by the University Grants Committee and its
subcommittees, comprised in large part of co-opted academics. So while central government directly controls the
operational functions of allocating resources and approving
new developments, it shares or delegates the normative
task of monitoring institutional standards and assessing the

quality of courses and units in order to earmark specific sums
for specific institutions.

Government itself, within the wider framework of public
policy, makes its own judgements not only about the number
of places to be provided in higher education, but also about
the capacities, both quantitative and qualitative, of different
types of institutions to meet those demands. Its judgements
can have a major impact on the shape and structure of the
system. It was governmental decisions which led to the
creation of the polytechnics and their endowment with particular constitutional characteristics, in the hope that certain
social and educational results would follow. The government,
through the Department of Education and Science, was also
responsible for the reduction and reconstruction of the
teacher training system.

As we have noted, however, within these global decisions
about how resources should be divided between different
sectors of the system, detailed judgements affecting individual
institutions are shared with or delegated to the central authorities for the higher education system. The Council for
National Academic Awards (CNAA) validates degrees and
other qualifications in the public sector. The CNAA operates
on peer judgements and does not involve any governmental
mechanism in deciding where academic merit lies. In the universities, judgements on academic quality are also left entirely
to peer review – though they are not institutionalised through
the central authorities, except in so far as they have a direct
bearing on UGC decisions about which institutions and basic
units deserve special support.

The arrangements for validating functions – to be separated
from those for overall resource allocation – seem to respond
to similar conventions in other areas of public activity. The
control over substantive content in medicine, social work
and other 'professional' areas is always allocated to inter-
mediary bodies (such as the General Medical Council or
the Central Council for Education and Training in Social
Work) administering different degrees of peer control but
backed by legislation enabling them to license practitioners,
or by royal charters giving them legal autonomy. In higher
education, this delegation implies particular value orientations on the part of government. Not only does it locate

within the central authorities judgements of academic quality and control depending largely on peer review, it also gives varying degrees of autonomy to institutions and basic units to initiate change and to promote decisions affecting the overall direction of higher education.[6]

The Sponsorship of Research

The central authorities within the higher education system use different lines of negotiation in respect of teaching and research. Research is implied rather than specified as an element of funding in the general resource allocations made to institutions. Staffing levels, building, equipment allowances, discretion to give sabbatical leave, are all evidence of inbuilt provision for research. But they are directly associated with, and are indeed a residue of, provision for teaching.

Research is financed in a variety of ways. First, five research councils, established under royal charter and operating by peer review, receive funds from which they distribute research grants and studentships within broad policies agreed with government. Second – as we have noted above – the two main channels of finance to institutions, through the UGC and through the local authorities, include indirect provision for research. Third, central government provides additional research funding through contracts negotiated with institutions and basic units for specific pieces of work: this mode is adopted, too, by industrial sponsors. Lastly, further marginal sums can be obtained from private foundations, who tend to use their funds as 'risk money' on projects considered to be more innovative or unorthodox than those which attract support from the research councils, or on proposals which are unrelated to – and perhaps critical of – government policies.

The value assumptions of individual academic inquiry, or of collaborative investigation of 'pure' research topics, rarely come into conflict with the other norms of institutions and basic units. Contract research, whether sponsored by government or industry, is however a different case. Its rapid growth has had discernible effects on the relationships between individuals, basic units, institutions and the central authorities. The central authorities may note with favour that a particular institution encourages its basic units to engage in research activities compatible with social needs. The peer groups to which such units belong may take the contrasting view that too close a relationship with the field of action is deleterious to academic standards.

The creation of what Don Price has called 'the scientific estate'[7] seems to have had different effects in different countries. Price concludes that far from subordinating the institutions or basic units to government, US sponsoring of research has strengthened the academic community's ability to enter into policy-making. It has been able to do so, both for its own and for the general benefit, without any noticeable weakening of its autonomy or its ability to sustain its own norms. In Britain, however, the publication of the Rothschild Report,[8] in which it was declared that government should seek to develop research through adopting a customer role from which contracts would be given, has led to considerable uncertainty about the implications for the academic enterprise. Fears have been expressed about a loss of integrity and independence for academic research; at the same time government, in the few statements it has made, has remained sceptical about the ability of the research institutions to meet social needs.

The research networks, both those developed by central government interests and those relating to the research councils, depend in large measure on academic judgements of the viability and validity of research proposals. Although the membership of such networks may well differ from that of the networks which advise on teaching resources, the problems and principles are much the same. Thus, central government, even in its grants to the independent research councils, increasingly gives indications as to the economic and social considerations to be met. At the same time, however, it would never interfere with the academic evaluation of whether a particular proposal for research is acceptable or not.

The Authority of the Centre and the Power of the Peer Groups

We have already alluded to the ambiguity of the academic peer groups' structural position within higher education. Some of their leading members are co-opted to the central authorities to assess the academic promise of the relevant basic units; at the same time, they are expected to contribute to authoritative decisions, delegated by government to the central authorities, on the allocation of institutional resources. Here we may note the caveat expressed by Burton R. Clark that 'it is better to assume that order is variously determined, rather than produced by administration alone'.[9] In many higher education systems, he writes, there are national and centralized bureaucracies: but 'always underneath that superstructure which lodged power in ministerial hands, there was the understructure of guild-like faculty units which lodged local power in professorial hands'.

It is also useful to note the distinction made by Robert O. Berdahl[10] between procedural and substantive autonomy. The first relates to the way in which universities are allowed to spend public funds; the second concerns such academic issues as teacher appointments, the selection and qualifying of students, and research programmes. The Berdahl distinction emerges in our model in a somewhat different form. Academic autonomy is represented as the ability of the basic units to maintain their peer-group norms and values and to judge individual standards while conforming to institutional requirements. In our model, too, the institution itself has power to maintain academic regulations and processes and to promote development while conforming to central demands. These freedoms in the normative mode have their operational counterparts in the freedom to allocate internal budgets so as to ensure that the curricula and research maintained by the basic units conform to the needs of the institution as a whole. In any event, as Rune Premfors and Bertil Östergren have pointed out,[11] the use of the word 'autonomy' in higher education needs to be limited in terms of who enjoys autonomy from whom and about what.

Relationships Between Central Authorities and other Levels

In principle, there are three ways in which a central authority may relate to the system for which it is responsible. The first is by adopting a managerial approach in which the central authority gives instructions, allocates resources to specific ends, and rewards and punishes according to the degree of conformity to its instructions. This is not a pattern accepted in most higher education systems, though it is widely familiar in industry and in some governmental R and D programmes. The second approach relies on a sizeable measure of consensus on functions, objectives and processes, so that prescription is unnecessary, and unconditional grants can be given for new developments. This free grant pattern was prevalent in a number of countries before higher education became an acknowledged component of social planning and a major charge to the public purse, but no longer obtains in most of them. The third strategy rests on an acceptance that there are divergencies of values and hence that there have to be negotiations between the various components of a pluralistic system. In our view this pattern is the only one that has any obvious relevance to contemporary higher education. As we have noted, however strong the bureaucratic system may appear, the professional guild or some other peer grouping remains potent.

Reliance on a negotiative pattern follows recognition of what is appropriate and possible. The four objectives of higher education described earlier in this chapter emerge as different tasks and in different mixes at the different levels of the system. The central government must be primarily concerned with the provision of suitably qualified manpower while the main emphasis of the basic unit, although certainly affected by social and economic norms, is on academic responsibility and the development of specialized knowledge and skills. It must follow, then, that while the institutions and the basic units move in response to government demands, they do so on the understanding that academic norms will not be adversely affected by such demands. The negotiations are not overt. There is nevertheless a strong implied theme running between the central authorities and the institutions, to the effect that academic freedoms over curriculum generation and maintenance and over research activity can be sustained as a *quid pro quo* for the institution's responses to national needs.

Examples of Negotiation
Within the system there are constant needs for development. We shall consider two examples. The first is the evolution of a unitary or comprehensive system, mainly involving a change in the operational mode; and the second, the modification of

traditional objectives, starting from a change in the normative mode.

A key feature of the emergence of a comprehensive higher education system in Britain, as elsewhere, has been the notion of inter-institutional planning and co-operation. The UGC and the DES consult each other about developments within regions or areas. The degree of detail with which they do so is not known, although on some issues, such as the future of teacher education within the private and public sectors, joint planning is fairly stringent.

The ideal of a comprehensive network of higher education institutions goes back as far as Haldane[12] and has been strongly reiterated in the era of the binary system by the representatives of the local authorities. Whatever the merits of such an idea, co-operation of this kind is intrinsically difficult to achieve, given the nature of academic autonomy. The basic unit is powerful in its resilience because it contains practitioners who are licensed to research and to teach freely, and because good academic development is essentially seen to be an extension of their motivation and abilities. It thus follows that central government's attempts to induce co-operation have had to follow in the wake of, rather than being able to predicate, the sanctioning of resources for particular purposes in individual institutions. No basic unit is told that it will get financial support only if it co-operates with units elsewhere.

This brings us back to Clark's point that order is variously determined. As he points out[13] the operationally meaningful goals of academic systems have to be shared between the disparate operational parts, unless they are to be fought out between them. Across some national systems the state may act as a co-ordinative authority. Or co-ordination might be effected by academic oligarchs or intermediate bodies whom he typifies as 'a form of structured pluralism in co-ordination'. But it is by no means clear whether those countries which have attempted to reduce the power of the professoriate have at the same time effectively weakened the discretion of the basic units and enhanced the authority of the central institutions.[14]

If one difficulty in systemic development is that of developing a form of co-ordination which enables resources to be used more economically, then a second is that of revising the functions of higher education as student numbers decline and as the demands for higher education become more various. The DES discussion paper on higher education into the 1990s provides a case in point.[15] Although essentially an ephemeral attempt at developmental planning, it is important because the department boldly argued that the present sources of demand for higher education were likely to falter, and suggested that higher education would do well to broaden the range of its activities, particularly to cater for the large untapped market of under-educated adults.

This DES initiative is a further illustration of how it is possible for government to specify the changes that might be needed if the production functions of higher education are to remain relevant to social and economic needs. It is also likely to demonstrate, however, that central planning faces obstinacies deriving from the nature of the academic enterprise and the institutions which participate in it. The primary resources in higher education — specialist manpower and buildings — are not easily manipulated to meet far-reaching changes in objectives. A system in which there is a striking emphasis on individual division of labour, on the pursuit of personal excellence and of individual creativity, is virtually unplannable, especially when there is no growth. Academic buildings incorporate educational and social purposes and assumptions which may not be consistent with new modes of teaching and social interaction. A higher education teacher who has spent, perhaps, ten years becoming skilled in a specific discipline or a particular area of knowledge and who has, moreover, always been told that his freedom is important both to the academic enterprise and to the maintenance of the democratic way of life, is not easily converted to new types of student groups, or new patterns of teaching, learning and research — particularly when these demands derive from the outside. That is not to deny that academics themselves initiate changes. Business studies, biochemistry, computer science, women's studies, have all developed from within academe.

Governmental Planning
Both these examples — of establishing a comprehensive

structure, and of diversifying the functions of the system — raise questions not only about the theory of planning but about the way in which the government as a whole — and by delegation the central authorities — might behave in the face of what are considered to be pressing social and economic needs. One possible approach is clearly consistent with negotiation — namely, that in which traditional patterns are modified to meet new circumstances, in response to market demands or to direct government pressure. In, for example, the development of master's courses (a form of provision not known before 1945), the mode has been negotiative, perhaps even consensual. Other innovations, too, have been triggered off by changing trends in the student market rather than by national prescription, but have been accepted by the central authorities as appropriately meeting social need. The central authorities could in principle choose simply to allow institutions and basic units to respond to market pressure, operating on the basis that where student demand is least resources would be withdrawn or reduced.

However, an incrementalist approach of this kind would be inconsistent with the two forms of planning — labelled respectively, 'manpower' and 'second generation' — that have predominated in recent years. Central planners are still, on the whole, 'first generation' or synoptic and rationalistic in their ambitions, while recognizing how difficult it is to get right the demographic and economic components of long-range forecasting, and to reconcile those calculations one with another. At the same time they are bombarded with demands for participation from all the potential stake-holders in policy-making, and particularly those representing the academic and political interests of practitioners. Second-generation planning attempts to take account of the impact of plans on those affected and of their views within the planning process.

Manpower planning rests on the assumption that it is at least in some sense possible to sum up the totality of national needs, and to plan accordingly. The strategies it advocates can be seen as shot through with the technocratic optimism of the late 1960s. As part of that rapidly discredited movement of thought, rational manpower planning has come under increasing criticism in recent years. But the agencies of government are unlikely to give up the attempt, even if public expectations would so allow, to relate the financing of higher education to the perceived needs of industry and society. On those grounds alone, a simple obeisance to student demand would not be feasible.

The mode of approach called imprecisely 'second-genera-tion' planning[16] seeks to take account of multiple states of mind. The taxpayers, the managers of the economy, the schools who supply the bulk of students, the teaching staff in higher education, the students themselves, all have different perspectives on the higher education enterprise. But the planning agencies, though in theory answerable to all of these, are in practice able to work more comfortably from the Treasury and governmental dimensions of managing the economy than as brokers between the different stake-holders in higher education.

Second-generation planning, properly conducted, would not allow student demand and the academic system's response to it to dominate planning calculations. Somewhere within the system authoritative decisions based on aggregates, no matter how crudely obtained, would still have to be made. The negotiative style does, however, introduce two reserva-tions into authoritative decision-making. First, it requires those who make decisions overtly to take account of the points of view of all with direct concern for higher education. Second, it requires government to be more openly participa-tive in the sense that, at minimum, it will explain its reasoning, openly seek public comment on what it does, and be prepared to defend its decisions. This further entails a sensitivity to the impact of policies made centrally, difficult though they are to predict.

To maintain a necessary degree of credibility, the govern-ment and its delegated authorities have to acknowledge and act upon the impact their decisions make. When, for example, staffing ratios are reduced, whether through direct prescrip-tion or through changes in levels of funding, certain con-sequences can be expected to follow within the basic units and the institutions. The balance between research and teaching might shift. Teaching might become less dependent than before on original research, and more dependent on set textbooks. The size and nature of teaching groups might change. The pastoral commitment of staff might be lowered. Or, to take another example, decisions to amalgamate institutions for the sake of economy or so as to create stronger and more varied institutions also have unexpected effects. The internal organization of an institution changes as it becomes larger. Inevitably the mechanisms for co-ordination and for the allocation of resources, as well as those for internal management in general, become more elaborate and take on lives of their own. The proportions of time spent on committee and other administrative work, and on the leadership of research and teaching, tend inexorably to increase. The career patterns of academics change. Morale among the staff of the assimilated institutions may sink to a low ebb. There can in some instances be a debilitating loss of identity and purpose.

It is not always easy to predict the impact of decisions made at the centre. The planners who expanded higher education in the 1960s could not reasonably have been expected to foresee all the changes that eventually took place — although some, certainly, could have been inferred from American experience. Our model is designed in part to bring out the social and educational impact of changes in different parts of the system, and to help in the analysis of policy. But the greater clarity of expectation to which the model can give rise is not normally to be found either in the pronouncements of public authorities or in the academic literature on higher education.

Styles of Governability
However we conceptualize the relationships embodied in planning, it remains the case that where government provides the large majority of funds, there is likely to be conflict on the ways in which economic and social desiderata are converted into institutional forms. Each of the major postwar initiatives, in advancing equality of access, and in gearing higher education to the economy, have caused major displacements. There have been changes in the status of professors, in the types of students who are admitted to higher education, in the balance between teaching and research, in staffing ratios, in the quality of buildings provided, in relative salaries. As we have shown, these changes

in the central authorities' norms have not only affected their allocative decisions but have also changed the institutional environments in which the norms of the basic units are formulated.

If the agencies of government deal with 'free' institutions they nevertheless expect outcomes, even if their expectations are not specific. The first grants made by the British Treasury to the universities seemed to be absolutely unconditional, but even then were made in the expectation that if the universities could produce well-educated people, socially beneficial results would ensue. (There was at the time, of course, no attempt to relate that desideratum to overall planning objectives, and indeed there were no mechanisms — nor even a language — with which it could be done.)

Higher education is an expensive and politically sensitive area of public investment. Not only its costs but also its potential outcomes are important to the national interest. As we have seen, much of the important norm-setting takes place away from the central authorities. They nevertheless take a view on even the best-guarded activities of individual teachers and basic units: but because the mode is negotiative, they will always fall short of prescribing directly. This duality sharply challenges the potential for national planning.

The complications of governability extend beyond the level of the basic unit, to the individual member of staff. The problem is that every teacher is expected to exercise his or her standards, even when working interactively with other individuals within the system. Society has traditionally expected its academics to be independent, although that tradition has to some extent been eroded by such considerations as the customer–contractor relationship between government and academic research, and by demands for 'relevance' from the student body and from others in the wider society. Even so, it should be noted that the government uses academics as consultants and committee members because it wants to have, or to be seen to have, independent judgement on some of its own activities. These are further reasons why the government has to negotiate, leaving aside any desire on the part of central authorities to be democratic or participative. This negotiative pattern leads to questions about the role of the institution in mediating between central authorities and the basic units. It is to such questions that we now turn.

5. The Institution

Is the Institution a Viable Level?
The academic institution is the principal legal entity through which most of the functions of higher education are performed. In terms of our model it is that body by which a group of basic units are authoritatively held together.

The model deployed in Chapter 2 and, indeed, much of the literature[1,2] have concentrated on three levels of authority and of value setting in higher education. Norms in higher education are often assumed to be determined either by single teachers or researchers within their basic units or nationally, in response to social and economic desiderata, by central authorities. This seems to leave the institution somewhat short of functions as a value-setter. Determining curriculum — a function of the basic unit — or determining whether an institution shall grow or stay still — a central authority decision in those countries in which central authorities exist — are substantive decisions. Mediating between the two seems to be secondary, non-substantive, almost intransitive, in the sense that the object of the exercise is at least one remove away.

Even if we accept the findings of Baldridge *et al.*, that the bureaucratic power of institutions is growing,[3] that still does not answer the question whether the institution is directly concerned with any of higher education's primary tasks. It remains to be considered how far the institution has a substantive existence and a distinct purpose or how far it is, in effect, a holding company, a legal and organizational formula designed to authorize activities extrinsic to itself.

An institutional level has to be defined in terms of whether it has discernible norms of its own; whether it performs discernible operations or tasks which are compatible with, if not in perfect fit to, those values; and whether it has authority to act in the normative mode by making evaluations of, and in the operational mode by making allocations to, its affiliated basic units and individuals.

The Two Faces of Leadership

The complex and ambiguous relationship of basic units and individuals to institutions emerges in such phrases as 'organized anarchy',[4] collegium, bureaucracy and 'federated professionalism'. All of these ascriptions have some truth in them, as have the two principal uncorrected versions of how institutions work.

The first, mainly held by those outside higher education — particularly as they view the almost total dependence on public funds of most higher education activities — assumes that institutions respond as unities to the leadership, if not the management, of a vice-chancellor or director. For all that they may acknowledge the complexities, the central authorities themselves act on the assumption that their requests, or guidance, or prescriptions, will be followed, provided that they only address themselves to a visibly nodal point of authority in an institution; and in fact, the chief administrator is nearly always able to secure a decision from his institution which matches the expectations of the funding body. Members of the public, too, may write to a vice-chancellor complaining of some statement made by an individual member of staff, or of the behaviour of a group of students, as if he can unequivocally exercise managerial authority. In this respect, however, the complainants are almost always disappointed.

A second uncorrected version rests on a denial of such internal authority as does exist. It represents the institution as being wholly collegial. This is a view traditionally sustained by members of academic staff, whose modes of working seem to be, on the face of it, antithetical to management, hierarchy or bureaucracy.

Both uncorrected versions reflect, between them, the Janus-like role of a vice-chancellor, principal or director; the dual systems of hierarchy and collegium running through the system; and the ways in which both individuals and committees themselves operate within hierarchy and collegium.

The Institutional Headship

The vice-chancellor is 'to most students and to some dis-affected staff . . . the very embodiment of "the administra-tion" . . . Yet almost all Vice-Chancellors to whom we have talked resent the label.'⁵ The vice-chancellor has dual expec-tations placed upon him. He is responsible for making sure that the institution sustains itself and, where possible, develops. Accordingly, he has to account for the way in which the university runs, both to its dominantly lay council and to the central authorities from whom he must seek funds. At the same time, he must lead and mediate among strongly idiosyncratic academics whose pre-eminence in their own professional spheres is likely to be among the institution's most important assets. The university vice-chancellor or polytechnic director is thus, at one and the same time, required to be a leader but also no more than the first among equals within his institution; an entrepreneur with external funders and — sometimes — within the university or poly-technic itself; an administrative service-giver to those who maintain the primary tasks and operations of the institution; a norm-setter, particularly for those operations not professed within the existing basic units; and, on rare occasions, an auto-crat exercising discipline on a wayward group of colleagues.

He is the key figure at all important committees, and the chairman of many. This gives him informal authority to veto proposals. He has the advantage of being entitled to attend any meetings he chooses and of being best informed about the total range of activities. He also has the moral authority of being able to assert a case for co-ordination to counteract the effects of idiosyncratic particularism. As we have noted, he is regarded from the outside as the most important figure in the institution. Internally, he occupies a pivotal position, particularly when there is competition amongst otherwise strong and ungovernable heads of the basic units. Yet with all this he is incapable of action except with the continuing support of the senate. In effect, he is possessed of great responsibilities but lacks the full authority to carry them out. Nevertheless, there is a sense in which to have responsibility itself confers a degree of power — it is rarely that a vice-chancellor is unable to persuade the senate on a matter in which his responsibility for the institution is in jeopardy.

These unusual characteristics of the vice-chancellor's role (which are less marked in the cases of polytechnic directors and college principals) derive from the fact that his shaping of the nature of the institution itself depends so heavily on the normative and operational authority of the basic units. It is from that factor among others that the overriding duality of hierarchy and collegium is derived.

The roles of vice-chancellors vary between universities and differ again from those of the directors of polytechnics or similar public sector institutions.[6] A vice-chancellor in a federal university certainly has a role different from that of a vice-chancellor in a unitary university. For example, university appointments, which are key points of control and development within any institution, are made by the colleges, basic units and the university faculties acting jointly. In other fields, too, there are interlocking powers and functions. For example, an Oxbridge or London college has purchase on its own development, on buildings and student numbers, but the university mediates UGC and other external fundings to the different disciplinary systems and to the colleges, apart from such private endowments as they might find themselves. The vice-chancellor and university administration thus have to act as brokers between heads of houses, the university faculty and the basic units within the colleges. The leadership (let alone the managerial function) is less clear-cut than in a unitary institution.

Public sector institutions are different again, although they vary amongst themselves. The central directorate is stronger and the academic boards are correspondingly weaker than their university counterparts. The local authority holds the director accountable for the running of the institution. This may strengthen his position in relation to the basic units. Faculties or schools are often larger and more heterogeneous in function than their university equivalents. Deans are often full-time administrators, working in hierarchical relationship to the director, and less likely to occupy the role of a convenor of colleagues than do some heads or chairmen of university departments, schools or faculties. It remains to be seen whether hierarchy will become weaker in public sector institutions as the basic units get stronger.

In all three cases — unitary, federal university and public

sector institutions — the components of collegium and hierarchy are present. The balance between each may, however,
vary, and the resulting styles may be entirely different.

Collegium and Hierarchy, Committee and Executive

The relative emphasis between hierarchy and collegium
changes over time, and varies between different types of institution. Hierarchy is the stronger element in traditionally
administered public sector institutions, but so it was in some
of the prewar civic and Scottish universities. The ancient
universities of Oxford and Cambridge have always been
strongly collegial, but a number of the newest foundations —
Sussex and East Anglia, for example — seem anxious to
outshine them in this respect.

Hierarchy assumes that the individuals in certain designated roles possess authority to affect the institutional
behaviour of others. Collegium designates a structure or
structures in which members have equal authority to participate in decisions which are binding on each of them. It
usually implies that individuals have discretion to perform
their main operations in their own way, subject only to minimal collegial controls (on, for example, the use of resources
and on the observance of proper procedures in the admission,
teaching and assessing of students).

Alongside the dual structure of hierarchy and collegium,
academic institutions contain systems of executive roles and
systems of committees. They seldom resolve the overlaps and
conflicts between them in any logical way. Within the executive structure itself, there are role relationships between the
head of an institution, the heads of basic units and individual
members of teaching staff. These are often quite elaborate.
There might be a vice-chancellor or director or principal,
deans of schools or faculties, heads of departments and
various role-holders such as senior tutors or admissions tutors
in basic units. This executive structure of (usually) part-time
academic managers is closely interlocked with the full-time
administrative system, nowadays usually staffed by career
administrators and headed by such senior permanent officials
as the registrar and bursar.

The equivocal status of the vice-chancellor is reflected in
roles lower down the executive hierarchy. Deans, for example,

may easily find themselves full of work and short of authority. They have to persuade basic units to make collective decisions which they can then put into action. Yet the unit heads are not their subordinates. They are equal in status and have an equal voice in the senate. The deans therefore have to exercise their leadership informally. Characteristically, they might work within small oligarchic mechanisms (such as deans' or heads of schools' meetings) and then assert their views collectively, with the support of the vice-chancellor, when matters arise in the senate or its committees. They may have to depend for the success of policies which they regard as in the collective interest, but which the basic units left to themselves would not agree, on being present at key meetings, on developing political expertise and on exercising it in all the committees to which they have access. At any one time, however, the decisions reached by deans can be changed or challenged within equivalent meetings of heads of basic units, or in the course boards at which members of basic units are in the majority, or in resource committees where the deans themselves may not be a dominant majority. So even their informal leadership may be exercised with difficulty.

Such lines of authority as exist as necessary parts of the academic executive structure are thus fragmentary and incomplete. The head of an institution has powers, although minimal ones, to act against a teacher or an administrator who is in serious default of duty. He can certainly influence the future of an individual member of staff by his intervention in the reward system which all institutions operate — but as against this, many of the academics with whom he has an executive relationship, such as the heads of basic units, will be at the peak of their profession, with tenure, and no particular wish for further advancement. The relationship between the head of a basic unit and an individual teacher within that unit is imprecisely defined and subject to negotiation. In the normal way, the contract of a tenured teacher merely states that he will work under the direction of the head of the basic unit, without further specifying the powers of that head and the duties of the teacher. For the most part, senior academics have the power to affect the rewards that the institution may give to its members, but virtually no power to impose sanctions of the kind usually attributed to a manager within any other kind of hierarchy.

The executive and administrative systems interlock in complex ways with the committee structure. The most senior committee — the council or equivalent body — always has a lay majority. Its powers over academic substance are minimal, although that has not always been so. In contrast, it has significant authority to sanction or restrict resources such as academic establishment, buildings and finance, although it will normally act here on the advice of the head of the institution. Its control over resources and its fiduciary role (through which it defends and monitors the general organizational behaviour of the institution) puts it into an equivocal relationship with the senate. That body, which consists wholly of academics, mostly senior, is the prime collegium in the institution. It may not set the normative modes by which the basic units work, but it prescribes and sanctions the frameworks within which the basic units formulate both their norms and their operations. It operates subordinate committees which carry effective executive powers, subject to reiterative scrutiny by the senate itself, on academic issues derived largely from the basic units. It also has committees concerned with planning and resources, through which peer control over allocations is maintained.

The primary mode of the committee system is collegial. However, just as the executive structure described above is not a pure hierarchy, so the committee network is not that of a pure collegium operating at different levels. In the first place, the more senior the committee, the more senior are the individual members of it. Much of the authority of, for example, a head of a basic unit derives from his membership of the senate. Second, many of the more important decisions are beyond the capacity of large bodies such as the council or senate to formulate, and so have to be hammered out in smaller and more informal groupings outside the collegial ethic.

The linking of executive with committee means that many individual roles are themselves dual. Thus a head of a basic unit, or the head of a faculty or a school (who is best thought of as a convenor of heads of basic units), operates both hierarchically, in as much as he possesses the power to direct and to affect the prospects of individual teachers, and collegially, in as much as he has to reach agreement with his colleagues on many of the major academic and allocative decisions.

The executive and the committee structures alike are thus shot through with both collegium and hierarchy. Moreover, as we have remarked, the relationships between the two can change as institutions go through different periods of history. When an institution is first set up, both its executive and its committee systems wield considerable power. Over time, institutions yield some of that power to the developing basic units, and some to the central administration.

Academies as Political Organizations

There is, then, in academic organizations, no rational allocation of tasks through a set system of roles in which the powers of managers are exercised over subordinates. Wherever authority exists, it may be held subject to collegial structures such as those of the senate, or of other influential groups, some of whose members may be quite junior within the academic executive system. The formal as well as the informal organization allows for the most important decisions to be the result of collegial procedures.

The interplay between executive and committee, hierarchy and collegium, cannot be easily rendered down into a straightforward and predictable structure. To understand the ways in which academic institutions function, we may need to consider other forms of analysis. One of these, developed by Baldridge *et al.*,[7] concentrates on political models of decision-making within higher education institutions. The research in question concludes that higher education is different from other enterprises in having more ambiguous and contested goals, in working with unclear technologies, in serving clients instead of working for profit, and in the fact that both the work force and the decision-making process are dominated by professionals.

Baldridge and his colleagues thus share the view of Cohen and March that academic institutions are not 'bureaucracies' but 'organized anarchies'. But within the organized anarchy decisions have to be reached, they contend, as the result of a political process in which various interest groups struggle for influence. This analogy between academic institutions and small-scale political entities (such as systems of local government) can be pursued in fair detail. To enumerate some of the important similarities, most individual constituents for most of the time, and some for all of the time, are not directly concerned in the shaping of policy. Allied to this, participation is fluid, in the sense that all but a politically committed few get involved only with particular issues over relatively short periods. As in the wider society, interests and loyalties tend to be fragmented, except in the case of internal schism or external threat. Value conflicts are a normal feature of the community; and, as we have seen, the degree to which direct authority can be exercised is very limited. Finally, the system is far from self-contained, being susceptible in a variety of ways to outside influences and pressures.

The political analogy has the advantage of embodying the twin conceptions of collegium and hierarchy, or community and organization, but going beyond them to account for the curiosities within academic institutions of policy-making and the exercise of power. The relationships are brought still more sharply into focus by F. G. Bailey's metaphor, in *Morality and Expediency*,[8] of the three arenas of academic discourse — front-stage, back-stage and under-stage. He points out that most of the public, permanent, large and representational committees in any institution exist to sanction decisions taken elsewhere, and to provide scope for ritualistic and high-minded assertions of value and purpose. This, the front-stage arena, embodies the institution's main political functions. The hard, detailed bargaining, designed to yield a working compromise, typically takes place in smaller, *ad hoc* or temporary groupings whose members are appointed or co-opted rather than elected. This, the under-stage arena, manifests the main organizational features of the institution. But the important tasks of forming alliances, making or breaking reputations, and creating a groundswell of opinion takes place back-stage, where the members of the scholarly community congregate to exchange their gossip.

The Functions of the Institution
The uncertainty which we expressed at the beginning of this chapter about the institution as a distinct level within higher education would seem to be reinforced by its ambiguities of

structure and modes of working. Yet decisions are certainly made — some of which may be of crucial importance to the welfare of the whole enterprise — which far transcend the concerns of any basic unit and clearly do not derive from the wishes of the central authorities. If the institution is not on first sight a national entity, it is none the less functionally indispensable. We now consider in more detail the place of the institution in our model (Figure 5.1), looking in turn at its normative and operational aspects.

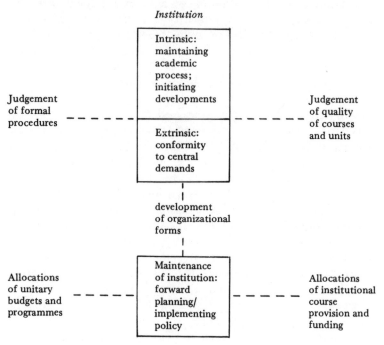

Institution

	Intrinsic: maintaining academic process; initiating developments	
Judgement of formal procedures		Judgement of quality of courses and units
	Extrinsic: conformity to central demands	

development of organizational forms

	Maintenance of institution: forward planning/ implementing policy	
Allocations of unitary budgets and programmes		Allocations of institutional course provision and funding

Figure 5.1 Functions of the institution

Normative Mode
In the normative mode, the institution relates its own assessments to central authorities' appraisals of the need for, and the quality expected of, particular courses and units. These central appraisals are informed by considerations of national economic and social needs and by views, usually based on peer-group judgement, on what constitute good academic standards. It is partly in reaction to such extrinsic demands

that the institution maintains academic regulations and develops the norms of academic behaviour expected of its component units. It also makes judgements of its own concerning the ways in which it can best meet the needs it perceives. The institution has a further fiduciary role. Its physical assets and its money income are seen as being held in trust for the pursuit of academic goals. This causes it to attend to the academic and the ethical reputation, as well as the financial probity, of work undertaken under its aegis.

It is recognized that the need to secure adequate balance between the different subject areas and between research, development and teaching activity is a proper institutional concern. In this connection, a view has to be reached on the proper relationship to be maintained with the community, and on how the enterprise as a whole should develop. Should it, for example, seek to resist or strive to accommodate to market pressures? Should it attempt to influence social and industrial practice by developing a strong technological emphasis, or should it seek to be a humanizing force by sustaining the long traditions of liberal education? Should it regard itself predominantly as a community of scholars or should it meet the demands of students and non-academic members of staff who seek a share in policy-making? These questions, though rightly expressed in the language of the normative mode, may nevertheless carry far-reaching operational consequences. For example, decisions to accept or ignore the market demand for courses necessarily affect the pattern of resources to be put into teaching and research.

Finally, the institution viewed in the normative mode must concern itself with due academic process. It is this set of norms that gives it the functions that can be described as rule-setting. A basic unit responsible for teaching and research in, say, physics or political science will be expected to recruit good physics or political science teachers and students. No other group within the institution has the expertise to do so for it. The institution nevertheless lays down rules by which recruitment is effected in accordance with general academic norms. It is important to recognize, though, that policies on such issues as the advertising of staff vacancies, or the need for external assessment of degree awards, are not *simply* rules: they incorporate values of institutional maintenance and standard-setting. They do not embody the same norms as those used by the peer groups in determining competence in physics or political science, but refer instead to such civic virtues as equity and due process. They are similar to the concerns which underlie the institution's fiduciary and reputational roles.

The problem remains whether the institution itself contributes distinctively towards the values within the higher education system as a whole. Three points might be made in this connection, deriving from the functions we have already distinguished within the normative mode.

First, we have already said that rule-setting involves institutional values such as those of maintaining equity and due process.

Second, there is the developmental function of assessing current operations against changing needs and environments. The institution must, in fact, look out for, initiate and nurture developments which are in the collective interest but lie outside the purview of the discipline-bound practitioner. The institution might think it right in a particular context to work more closely with the community, to take a more active role in civic change and development. At such a time, a vice-chancellor may have to lure a professor away from his laboratory or his study to listen to the expressed needs of local councillors or of industry. The institution may have to push through such 'unwanted' developments as the establishment of a new medical school, which would clearly disrupt the existing pattern of resource priorities, or a department of management studies, which all theoretical social scientists of pure heart would feel bound to resist, or a special engineering course, whose advent would not be taken kindly by those whose engineering was thus seen not to be 'special'.

In pursuing this function, the institution certainly takes on functions which are separable from those of any other level. It is the institution which acts as the point upon which external pressure is exercised. It also has to reconcile expectations of both the central authorities and the basic unit. At the same time, however, the institution draws strength from its relationship with outside authorities and sources of power.

In performing its developmental function an institution must have the capacity to seize opportunity quickly — a new course, or chair, or line of research — and, if necessary, to redistribute funds accordingly. The central authorities cannot move fast enough: moreover, they lack the knowledge of, and immediate control over, what is possible at the institutional level. The institution must also take a view on such matters beyond the concern of basic units as the total size of the institution; whether it should seek to be intimate and elite, or large and service-giving; whether it should, corporately, aim to cater for part-time and mature, perhaps not too well-qualified, students, or whether it should gear its courses to young full-time entrants with orthodox qualifications; and whether it should adopt particular modes of government, or forms of participation which seem likely to affect the pattern of relationships within the basic units themselves.

The third point about the institution as a distinctive level in the model concerns the creation of a public persona. Every university, polytechnic and college has to market itself, not only to potential recruits and to possible benefactors, but also to the polity at large. Some have done this brilliantly and others badly. Creating a reputation and earning general esteem is not a substantive task in its own right, but it helps to support and make more potent the main activities of an instititution. The task of image-building is partly achieved through ritual — the award of honorary degrees, the degree congregation, the public appearances of vice-chancellors and senior academics speaking not only on their specialist subjects but on the plight of humanity more generally. It seeks to reinforce the impression that while some departments might be excellent, and others pretty poor, the whole is a force for culture, knowledge and social development. The projection of such a view is clearly a task for the institution rather than the basic unit.

Operational Mode

The institution, in the operational mode, is shown as negotiating with and receiving allocations from the central authorities. It also develops the organizational forms, maintains the institution, allocates budgets and programmes to the basic units and undertakes forward planning.

The institution makes a case for resources and receives them from the central authorities and from other agencies.

In so doing, it collates and adjudicates between the demands of the basic units. But the institution's role is understated if it is regarded as no more than a mediator of its basic units' requirements. The central authorities build up judgements, not only about where individual subjects can best be advanced, but also about the total shape and size of individual institutions. An institution must therefore promote a view not only of its basic units but also of its total development, in a form which will be convincing to the central authorities. (In the past, institutions sought to convince private bene-factors or civic authorities in much the same way.)

Once it has resources of money, buildings and manpower, the institution distributes them to the basic units. Some criteria will be set, usually implicitly, by the central auth-orities, who will give 'guidance' on the balances to be struck between the different groups of disciplines, between post-graduate and undergraduate numbers, and so on. Within these general frameworks – or even ignoring them – institutions determine allocations either on the basis of such market in-puts as student demand for courses, or through the demands of other constituencies such as those interested in promoting particular forms of research. Universities (but not in this case the public sector institutions) also hold property, and have all the responsibilities of a large employer of academic and non-academic staff. They also have contractual and other relation-ships with students and are legal entities responsible in law for the decisions they make and the resources they employ.

The Outside Environment
Institutions work within a diversity of environments, some of which are given formal expression but many of which are not. The formally created relationship between a university and the laity is the council, sanctioned by royal charter and enjoying specific powers over the university's finance and resources. In some public sector institutions, governing bodies have responsibilities well beyond those accorded to university councils, and may be affected by the tenacity of members of a local authority in controlling the disposal of public money.

The functions and composition of councils and governing bodies again reflect various assumptions about the relationships between higher education and society.[9] Collegiate institutions may be entirely self-governing in that they hold monies in trust which they administer through their own college meetings of fellows. Non-collegiate universities are required to defer on all matters of finance, buildings and establishments to a council that may well be partly nominated by the vice-chancellor and members of academic staff but whose majority comes from groups specified by charter and deemed to represent different groups in society. Polytechnic governing bodies also comprise memberships laid down in their articles of government approved by the central authorities. The majority of members are appointed by the local authority.

The intensity of control and the balance of authority between council and senate, governing body and academic board, cannot be predicted from the formal statement of functions. Council and governing body have a fiduciary role over anything that smacks of resources. But resource allocations are a metaphor for the allocation of values. The extent to which it is academe, and the extent to which it is society (as represented by the lay majority body), which makes the running, is certainly variable and volatile.

Other environmental forces include the challenges posed by strong market demands for courses, the pressure put by professional licensing bodies on course boards in certain applied subjects, and the emphasis given to certain themes as a result of financial sponsoring from industry, commerce or the government. Baldridge[10] has shown how different institutional systems in the USA are affected by a variety of environmental relationships still relatively unfamiliar in Britain. The relationship between institutions and the political leadership of the community, the changing financial base as between private and public money, the changing pool of clients, the changing pattern of industrial relations and the unionization of different staff groups, the extent to which social decision-making is subject to the intervention of the courts — a characteristic strongly established in the USA, but growing steadily in the UK — all these are factors which could have an effect on the ways in which institutions behave.[11]

Integrity and Adaptability

The institution has to bring into working relationships the two main structures of hierarchy and administration, and of collegium and committee. The functions of each are never clearly delineated. Yet whatever the internal complexities, it is the institution that must ensure that the whole enterprise is seen to work, that it can negotiate resources, and that it can maintain status and reputation with the outside world of sponsors, potential students and central authorities.

In presenting competence to the outside world, the institution has also to display its ability to assimilate, if on its own terms, the values of the society which ultimately must sustain it. Strong institutions are those which comfortably adapt to, rather than keep aloof from, the external environment. They take on and are able to face challenges, both intellectual and social, from the outside. At the same time, their internal systems must be sufficiently flexible, through their use of hierarchical and collegial forms, to reach consensus on those questions of purpose and function which make the institution coherent and reliable in its external relationships. The institution must thus stand firmly on its own range of values but exhibit perviousness to the outside world.

One of the central functions of the institution is to set the style of decision-making and to define the total range of activities that its basic units will perform. Its decisions about the balance between collegial and hierarchical formats are in fact decisions, too, about the best ways in which to harness the individuals and basic units to the collective development without destroying their key role in norm-setting. In practice that balance may not always be satisfactorily achieved, as we shall see in Chapter 9.

6. Basic Units

The Nature of Basic Units

Any full understanding of how the higher education system works must depend on an understanding of the basic units which together comprise its constituent institutions. By basic units we mean the smallest component elements which have a corporate life of their own. Their identifying characteristics would normally include an administrative existence (a designated head or chairman, a separately accounted budget); a physical existence (an identifiable set of premises); and an academic existence (a range of undergraduate training programmes, usually some provision for graduate work and sometimes a collective research activity). A unit would not be regarded as basic, in our sense, if it contained within it two or more sub-units showing such characteristics (for example, a department of anatomy might constitute a basic unit, but a medical school would be an amalgam of a number of such units).

In traditional university structures, the basic unit would usually be taken as the individual subject department, rather than the faculty bringing together a number of cognate departments. However, this is not a hard-and-fast rule, since some long-established universities use the term 'faculty' where others would use 'department' (for example, as in 'faculty of economics' where there are no sub-units). Some more recent institutions have developed alternative structures, in which the constituent elements are more broadly based 'schools of study', 'course teams', and the like. Hence the need to use a neutral term, such as 'basic unit', in discussing the nature of the individual elements which make up the institution as a whole.

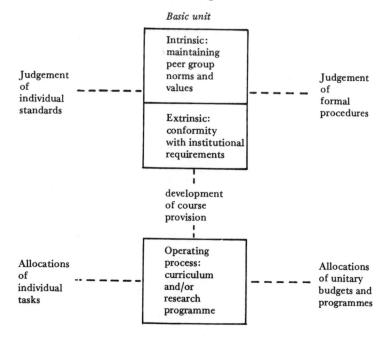

Figure 6.1 Functions of the basic unit

Basic units are especially important in the determination of professional values, and in the maintenance and development of particular areas of academic expertise.[1] Although they are by no means all alike in either their normative or their operational aspects, their main differences from one another can be charted along a relatively limited number of dimensions. Our first purpose here will be to identify the dimensions and to describe the range of variation which each can encompass. We shall want to suggest, among other things, that the subcultural styles and epistemological traditions to which particular teaching units subscribe are a powerful determinant of their relationships within and outside the institution, of the curricular patterns which they adopt in their undergraduate programmes, and of the nature of their day-to-day processes of teaching and learning.

Free-standing research units, projects or teams are another species of basic unit.[2] They differ in a number of respects from units which have a teaching function and lie somewhat outside the mainstream of academic activity. Overall, they form only a small proportion of the whole range of basic units. They often depend largely on external funds, and are liable to have a less permanent existence than teaching units; although generally directed by tenured academics, they are predominantly staffed by people on short-term contract; and — symbolically — they are almost invariably located on the periphery of the campus, or even outside it (typically, in a series of large converted Victorian houses). If their work is successful, they may earn the relevant disciplinary group, and the parent institution as a whole, much credit; but they do not thereby acquire greater political power. They are distributed unevenly as between pure and applied sciences, the social sciences and arts. Their place in institutions may perhaps change as government sponsorship of research becomes more prescriptive, and as the overall number of tenured posts remains static or declines. But the change is likely to be quantitative rather than qualitative.

The Research–Technology–Scholarship Triangle

The first analytic ascription to be made in characterizing basic units relates to where they lie within the triangle marked out by pure research at one apex, technology and the professions at another and academic scholarship at the third. The rough conventional distinctions between research, technology and scholarship can usefully be sharpened, for our present purposes, by allowing 'research' to connote only the pursuit of new knowledge, 'technology' (or 'professional study') to refer to the application of existing knowledge to practical purposes and 'scholarship' to designate the critical reappraisal of the corpus of existing material in any given field. In this specialized usage, a chemist investigating the hitherto unknown properties of a synthetic compound would obviously be doing research. The value of the work would be assessed in terms both of its originality and of its apparent importance in the development of the specialized field to which it contributed. An electronic engineer using the recently discovered properties of the same compound to develop a new computer circuit would, equally obviously, be engaged in technology. The same would be true of a specialist in business management applying the ideas of organization theory in developing a new structure for labour relations in industrial firms. In both these cases, the value of the work would again depend on its originality, but also on its likely usefulness and applicability in a wide range of circumstances. In contrast, a specialist in English literature might demonstrate his or her scholarship by offering a new interpretation of Marlowe's poetry. The originality of the critical analysis would once more be an important consideration; but its value would depend also on the author's mastery of the body of material under review, and the extent to which the interpretation was faithful to all the available evidence.

These deliberately sharpened contrasts, while useful in charting the field of academic values, are of course (like the contours on a map) a conceptual simplification of a less tidy reality. There are readily familiar cases in which chemists give up pure research but begin to apply the findings of others in a context which is clearly technological. There are electronic engineers whose interests take them away from the application of knowledge, but who maintain a mastery of developments in their specialism and subject it to critical analysis, in much the scholarly style ascribed in our example to the English literature specialist. Again, those engaged on literary pursuits do not always confine themselves to the reinterpretation of existing texts; on many occasions, they seek and discover new material from the archives or fresh bibliographical or historical data in a genre which can only be described as research.

The roles of researcher, technologist/professional or scholar, then, are not fixed or unchangeable: the careers of individual academics may shift between different roles at different stages. Nor are they capable of tidy allocation to practitioners in one academic domain rather than another. Even so, the terms can usefully serve to mark off the distinctions between the empirical quest for new data, the pragmatic translation of theory into practice and the predominantly analytic and reflective reordering of existing knowledge.

A number of basic units may themselves exist in a state of uneasy tension between two, or sometimes all three, of the different value systems which characterize these three categories of academic pursuit. But in other cases, the pre-dominant values of a basic unit will tend to be characterized by one approach to the exclusion of the rest, even where all three styles are possible within the same discipline. Some sociology departments might, for example, have a distinctly professional image, in their concern with social welfare; others might have a predominantly research image, concen-trating on the acquisition of field data; others again might emphasize scholarship and the development of interpretative frameworks. In other, longer-established disciplines, the connection with research, technology or scholarship will tend to be more stable or predictable. In a number of cases the very nature of the subject-matter would seem to set firm constraints on style. It would be surprising, for example, to find an astronomy department whose approach was mainly technological, or a school of tropical hygiene whose central interest was scholarly, or a philosophy department whose prime concern was with empirical research. Nevertheless, as we shall argue in Chapter 8, the configurations of subjects can and do alter and in so doing provide one powerful source of academic innovation.

Relationships Within and Outside the Institution

The reason for rehearsing (and even to some extent over-emphasizing) these familiar distinctions is that they play an important part in determining the characteristic norms and operations of basic units. In the normative mode, different types of units have different external reference groups; they tend to enjoy different degrees of academic prestige; and their work gives rise to different forms of extrinsic validation.

Research-oriented units, characteristically, draw profes-sional status and recognition from appropriate academic organizations in their own fields (the Royal Society, or at a more modest level the Royal Institute of Chemistry, or the British Psychological Association, as the case might be). The general academic prestige which derives from their field of activity tends to be high (with a few minor exceptions, such as the quantitative aspects of sociology). The rough-and-ready way in which particular units are assessed by colleagues in other fields tends to be in terms of the volume of research funding they attract. Nevertheless, research status as such rarely stems from any other source than peer-group review. It does not relate in any direct sense to nature of sponsorship or to promise of social or other utility (though once acquired, a good reputation in research does, as we remarked in Chapter 4, contribute to decisions by central authorities about budgetary allocations).

Somewhat different considerations apply to technologically or professionally based units. Their main recognition comes from professional bodies whose membership overlaps but is not coterminous with the academic world (the Royal College of Physicians, the Law Society, the Institute of Civil Engineers, and so on). Because these bodies are composed largely of practitioners, they tend in general to be less highly regarded than purely academic associations. By extrapolation, the prestige of technological and professional units within academia is generally lower than that of research-oriented ones.[3] (Two notable exceptions are law and medicine, whose high status derives partly from their antiquity and partly from their strength in attracting students.) The non-specialist's criterion for judging such units tends to be in terms of the extent to which they collectively, or their members individually, succeed in winning professional consultancies or in being called in to advise colleagues in the outside world.

While research-oriented and technologically or professionally based units seek recognition from associations of fellow academics or practitioners, units with a scholarly emphasis tend to identify individual peers as their points of external reference. The academic prestige of fields of scholarly activity again tends to be generally high. The common form of outside validation for units in this category is in terms of publication record, combined with an appraisal of their degree of collegial acclaim.

Turning now to the operational level, similar distinctions can be noted in terms of characteristic activities, levels of demand on institutional resources and credit ratings for undergraduate intake. Looking first at characteristic activities, the staff of research-based units usually work in a number of distinct groups, often on related problems, and will make extensive use of assistance from doctoral students or grant-aided researchers. Technological and professional units may adopt the same pattern for outside consultancy, but their members will in certain contexts act as individuals. The most common activities in units with a mainly scholarly emphasis are reading and writing, which are not often undertaken as collective pursuits.

The demand for resources from research-based units is usually high. In many cases this is because empirical inquiry in the discipline demands costly materials, or expensive apparatus, or both, together with laboratory space and research and technical assistance. Work which is field- rather than laboratory-based incurs costs of transport, residence, and the like. The pattern for technological and professional units is more variable. Obviously, engineering and medicine are high-cost activities, but law, social work and many other pursuits in this category are relatively inexpensive. Units devoted to scholarship commonly call for little more than adequate library facilities and so are low-cost in comparison with their research-based counterparts.

As far as student demand is concerned, the pattern is changeable and subject to all manner of extraneous market forces. Nevertheless, there is a *general* tendency for pressure for places to be low in research-based units, high in technological and professional ones (with occasional exceptions related to the job market) and mixed in scholarly oriented units (with English literature and history firmly at the upper end of the scale).

The Curriculum Matrix
At this point, another and rather different set of distinctions can be introduced. They are helpful in delineating certain characteristic curricular patterns in higher education, which in their turn influence the nature of basic units and the organizational structure of the institutions in which they are embedded. The first distinction marks the extent to which the boundaries of the subject-matter are strongly defined and guarded, as against the extent to which they are hospitable to considerations outside the strict disciplinary norms.[4] A curriculum with closed boundaries is one which firmly rules out the consideration of evidence other than that held to be directly related to the existing disciplinary framework; one which is permeable will allow for the importation of new, but extrinsic, ideas.

The second distinction concerns the degree of cohesiveness of subject-matter which is expected within the undergraduate curriculum, as opposed to the extent to which the component elements are permitted to be discrete and not necessarily linked at the conceptual level.[5] If the programme as a whole hangs together round a limited number of integrating themes, and there is a clear attempt to achieve intellectual unity, then it can fairly be described as cohesive. If it encompasses a range of separate and apparently unconnected components, where the links, if any, do not seem to be counted as important, then it can be designated as discrete. The two sets of distinctions — the one relating to the permeability of subject boundaries and the other to cohesiveness of content within those boundaries — can be brought together to form a four-cell matrix (Table 6.1).

Table 6.1 An outline matrix of curricular patterns

| | | Subject boundaries | |
		Closed	Permeable
Curricular content	Cohesive	1	2
	Discrete	3	4

Next, we shall identify the curricular patterns which best correspond with these four different pairs of characteristics. The first cell in the matrix, representing closed boundaries and cohesive content, is easy enough to allocate, since these are the familiar characteristics of single-subject specialist curriculum programmes. The third cell, similarly, defines a fairly common species of curricular pattern, namely, that in which a number of separate and self-contained thematic topics are pursued simultaneously, but with no special attempt to relate them to one another. Broadly based 'foundation courses', joint honours programmes and unit or modular degree schemes all fit into this pattern.

The second cell represents a relatively more recent development, namely, the emergence of interdisciplinary courses which are area-based or problem-based rather than related to conventional disciplines (examples would include courses in urban development or European studies). In such courses, a considerable effort is made to develop a sense of unity between the various disciplinary components: but the boundaries of the course remain permeable to new elements, provided only that these have some acceptable degree of relevance to the central theme.

Finally, the fourth cell seems best to correspond with some of the more recent conceptions of open learning, lifelong study or *education permanente*. It implies an ability for the student to select individual items of curricular content at will, but not to be subject to the discipline-based restrictions that characterize modular degree programmes. It depends on the notion of cumulative and transferable credit, negotiated in relation to approved pieces of work over a relatively unrestricted time-span. The curriculum of the 'University Without Walls' in North America may provide perhaps the best-known example of this pattern. (The Open University in the UK does not, since it operates in an interdisciplinary fashion at the foundation level and in a modular fashion at the more advanced levels.)

The completed matrix, with examples of curricular patterns included, therefore emerges as shown in Table 6.2.

Table 6.2 Some varieties of curricular pattern

| | | Boundaries | |
		Closed	Permeable
Content	Cohesive	Single-subject specialized degrees	Interdisciplinary courses
	Discrete	Modular or joint course schemes	Open learning programmes

It now remains to consider what seem to be the most appropriate organizational frameworks to match these different curricular patterns, and to look briefly at the possible consequences of a mismatch.

Curricular Patterns and Academic Structures
As far as an ideal framework can be found for a single-subject degree, it is surely the traditional specialist department.

This offers a complete correspondence of interest between academic organization and teaching commitment, with the department identified in terms of the specialized subjects it teaches and its staff and students sharing the same clear sense of discipline-based identity.

However, the departmental structure is less appropriate to a modular degree scheme. Individual departments will often tend to compete amongst themselves for student numbers, using a variety of ingenious, but not always educationally productive, tactics. They may also introduce unnecessary rigidities in the system by insisting on a series of prerequisite courses, or complicate matters by keeping to their own marking schemes. In practice, those UK institutions which have gone farthest in the direction of modularizing their courses have tended to move to a structure in which course teams provide the organizational basis for teaching and subject groups provide the basis for research. Each course team consists of all the staff involved in teaching a given unit or module. Its success is determined largely by the degree to which the particpants work effectively together. An individual member of staff will normally belong to two or three course teams, but in most cases to only one subject group. The course teams often have their own budgets, so that they form in effect a basic unit in the terms earlier defined.

Just as the traditional academic structure has had to be modified to accommodate modular degrees, so too it has proved clearly unsuitable to interdisciplinarity. The problem stems from the tendency of discipline-based groups to lay unique claim to certain areas of knowledge and to close off attention to what lies beyond their own professional boundaries. This parochialism is exactly what the advocates of interdisciplinary courses set out to avoid. In general, they can only succeed if they manage to by-pass or break down the departmental framework. This has commonly been done in UK universities by reorganizing the whole structure of the institution in terms of schools of study. These schools are then taken to constitute the basic units within the institution, each devoted to the broad theme which forms the subject-matter of its own degree programme or programmes. Thus one such school might be designated English and American studies; another environmental science; and so on.

The sectional interests of particular subject disciplines are, in theory, if not always in practice, subjugated to the wider requirements of interdisciplinary teaching and research.

Finally, open learning programmes of the type outlined earlier must clearly call for a much more flexible and open structure than any of those so far discussed. Indeed, they appear almost to transcend traditional notions of structure, much as some modern painting, poetry and music would seem to do. But in practice they involve the creation of relatively informal and shifting networks of co-operating institutions and individuals. Thus, in such a system, a given student might spend six months working full-time on an individual study project on transportation management at Polytechnic A, to earn two credits; work part-time for the ensuing year on a single-credit course on urban geography at University B; follow this after a year's interval by embarking on a two-year part-time programme on advanced network analysis, carrying three credits, at Polytechnic C; and so on. Programmes of this kind represent a new area of academic growth. They are not so much extra-instructional as inter-institutional. Although they may well in the long run modify existing organizational forms at the level of the basic unit, their immediate impact has been on the relationships between different institutions and the structure of the system as a whole.

We have attempted here to show how different curricular patterns call for different types of academic structure, often modifying the way in which an institution's basic units are defined. In terms of our model, a significant change in the predominant academic values of the peer group leads to a comparable change in the nature of the operating process at the level of the basic unit. This change can conflict with the existing mechanisms at the institutional level and lead to an imbalance between the normative and operational modes. The conflict has eventually to be resolved either by a final refusal on the institution's part to collaborate, or by organizational reform — unless it happens that the institution already has some appropriate mechanism to accommodate structural developments.

Transactions Between Basic Units
Even at the level of fairly modest transactions between basic

units, not involving ambitious modular schemes or inter-disciplinary degree programmes, troubles frequently arise by either horizontal or vertical departures from the accepted norm of the single-subject curriculum in our matrix. Horizontally, attempts to open subject boundaries slightly to incorporate materials from other disciplines, in the form of 'service' courses, run into one particular kind of difficulty. Vertically, moves to widen introductory programmes by pooling an initial intake of students between different basic units run into a different set of snags.

The generally unsatisfactory nature of service courses in higher education is widely acknowledged — that is, courses in which one basic unit is commissioned to provide a limited amount of introductory or remedial teaching for students in another (chemistry for biologists, say, or statistics for socio-logists).[6] The main problem derives from differences between the values of the two units involved in such a transaction. The host unit's natural concern is with the integration of the new material into the texture of its own curriculum. It has a largely instrumental view, seeing the exercise as a relatively marginal one in which elementary techniques are to be ac-quired and basic factual material assimilated by students in the minimum possible amount of time. The guest unit, on the other hand, is generally anxious not to seem to be under-mining the integrity of its discipline by portraying it as nothing more than a disconnected set of tools and topics. Its staff show some reluctance in taking on what is seen to be a low-prestige task, and become the more prone to emphasize their disciplinary dignity.

The result of this divergence of emphasis, from integration on the one hand to integrity on the other, is often a course which neither the host nor the guest unit regard as having much value. It will normally, as a necessary chore, be taken on in rotation, if not simply delegated to the most junior members of the guest unit. There will therefore be little continuity of staffing from one year to the next. In any event, the guest staff will tend to be given a sketchy briefing of what is required, and comparably limited academic support, from their colleagues in the host unit. Their own unit will tend to allocate the minimum reasonable amount of preparatory time for the task. There will thus be neither opportunity nor incentive to integrate the outside material with the rest of the curriculum.

In defence of their own and their subject's reputation, the guest staff will be driven to emphasize underlying principles, largely at the cost of applications relevant to the host discipline. They will accordingly demand from students a greater degree of academic commitment than the students (reading the signals emanating from their own units) could realistically be expected to give. The students themselves will usually fail to understand the purpose of the exercise, or its connections with their main programme. They will in many cases soon find themselves out of their depth in coping with an unfamiliar theme, and will withdraw from all but the necessary minimum of involvement.

In contrast with this sequence of mutual failures of adjustment characteristic of service courses, other hazards beset those basic units which combine to provide multi-subject introductory programmes. The common purpose behind such programmes is thoroughly well intentioned — as it is with service courses. It is based on two considerations. The first is that students who are unfamiliar with a broad, general field should have an opportunity at least to sample the range of disciplines it covers before they are required to make a final choice within the field. The second is that even where students have already made such a choice, it is useful for them to be able to see their own specialism against the background of neighbouring areas of inquiry.

Programmes based on these considerations usually take the form of first-year or first-semester schemes covering between two and four subjects, the students being expected to select the subject or subjects for specialized study at the end of this period. Normally, the time allocation for all subjects is the same within the programme, so that problems of primary and secondary (host and guest) partnership do not arise. Nor is there usually any aspiration towards, or expectation of, framing connections between component elements: the conflict between integration and integrity is also avoided. Each participating unit is of equal standing with the rest and each is expected to devise its own self-contained introductory course.

This very equality of status can create its own problems.

When the incoming students are admitted on the basis of primary allegiance to a particular basic unit, that unit will understandably display a possessiveness about its own recruits at the expense of those attached to other units. The common concern will be to keep hold of one's own students and with luck recruit a few more from rival units. Special academic or social activities may be laid on, over and above those provided within the framework of the programme. Unit-based activities will be played up, and inter-unit ones played down. This progressive weakening of the original framework will have its effect on students, who will be found to complain that the broadening element at the start of their course fails to fit in with the rest, introduces extraneous and irrelevant material, takes up unnecessary time and deserves to be abolished. Thus schemes of this kind, based on an 'indentured' intake, are liable slowly to atrophy.

Other such schemes are run with 'free' students — that is, ones admitted with a firm expectation that significant numbers of individuals may change their initial preference after completing the introductory programme. Here the endeavour to win the hearts and minds of students can become even more competitive. There is over time a tendency for each participating unit to expect rather more commitment of interest and attention from students than they might devote to the other units, and hence a growing student workload which can eventually lead to disaster. Although in general the competition is kept within decent limits, accepted behaviour being defined by the collective norms of the institution, there can be instances in which one basic unit is deemed by the others participating in the programme to have overstepped the mark. To give one instance, one participating department succeeded in introducing a group project into its part of the scheme, with the predictable result that the students devoted an undue share of their time and effort to working on this. The scheme in question was eventually disbanded as no longer functional.

These examples of relationships between basic units have been considered at some length, because they help to illuminate the way in which differences at the normative level between one unit and another can give rise to problems at the operational level in relation to shared curricular activities.

At this point we shall leave the issue of relationships between basic units and look at a value distinction whose implications are mainly internal to the basic unit itself.

The Positivist–Relativist Axis

The contrast between positivist and relativist approaches which now needs to be made, like those that preceded it, is deliberately sharpened for clarity. We do not want to suggest that, in practice, every basic unit is exclusively defined by one or other set of properties: the real world is a good deal less tidy. But the properties themselves are clearly distinguishable, and represent important differences in world view and attitude to knowledge.

We start by concentrating on those subject areas where it is possible, in principle at least, to maintain that the processes and outcomes of inquiry are independent of their social and historical context. These are, by definition, the domains of academic activity in which truth can be regarded as absolute, and in which knowledge rests on a bedrock of proof. Basic units which satisfy these epistemological principles we shall label as occupying the positivistic end of the scale which now concerns us.

At the other extreme, we focus on those intellectual pursuits in which there can be no possibility of maintaining that the processes and outcomes can be separated from, or evaluated outside, their social and historical context. Here it necessarily follows that truth has a relative rather than an absolute status, and knowledge depends on the development of a refined judgement rather than on incontrovertible demonstration. In terms of our scale of contrasts, basic units whose intellectual activities exhibit such properties in a pure form would be located at the relativistic end of the continuum.

So far, the difference which has been sketched out has been limited to the immediate consequences of logically different forms of academic inquiry. If the analysis is correct, all that follows is that the basic units which embody one or other of such forms of inquiry — or indeed, those which combine the two in differing proportions — have a certain set of intrinsic characteristics (to do with whether they suppose their activities to be cumulative, how much they attend to matters of time and place, how they assess academic excellence, and the like). What we might usefully do at this point is to extend the analysis by drawing attention to some purely contingent but nevertheless fairly common consequential features of units with a positivistic bias on the one hand and those with a relativistic bias on the other.

Beginning as before with the positivist position, we may infer that, since proof occupies a central place in the intellectual framework, one of the prime considerations in teaching must be to develop in students the capability for reaffirming proven results, and perhaps eventually proving new ones for themselves. The natural means to this goal, since proof both depends on and generates knowledge, is to ensure that a carefully selected body of subject-matter is presented to students and learned by them. The choice of this corpus of curricular material is not considered to be arbitrary. Moreover, the intellectual hierarchy is understandably defined by competence in validated discovery and the extensive knowledge on which that depends. The student at the bottom of the hierarchy can best rise up it by unquestioningly assimilating the required knowledge and obediently reiterating the already established proofs. One might say that being initiated into a positivist pursuit characteristically demands that one becomes the passive recipient of a body of knowledge identified and handed down by those in authority.

In direct contrast, relativist units give pride of place to the notion of judgement. So in such units it would naturally be seen as important to enable students to develop the necessary judgemental skills. In order to do so they must steep themselves in the methodology and style of argument characteristic of the field in question, and this means constant practice in applying that methodology and reaching judgements on their own initiative. Curricular content exists predominantly to provide the raw material for the exercise of interpretive insight: it is not considered to have any major intrinsic value, and the actual syllabus of topics is usually acknowledged to be a product of its particular context (its relativity being signalled by allowing students a wide choice of options). There will often be a comparatively weak sense of hierarchy in such units, with respect being accorded to those who have demonstrated the capacity for sound and scholarly appraisal. The student progresses best by learning to ask sensible critical questions, practising his skills in marshalling evidence and advancing arguments, and interacting in a direct and personal way with those who teach him. The initiation process into a relativistic field of inquiry thus typically calls for the novice actively to engage in developing a methodology — and hence to acquire understanding and sound judgement — with his teachers acting as his exemplars and his coaches.

We remarked earlier that these operational distinctions were contingent, rather than necessary, consequences of the normative contrasts between basic units with particular sets of intrinsic characteristics. It is possible, and does indeed happen from time to time, that a basic unit where inquiry can be represented as context-free elects not to so regard it, and chooses, in its teaching, to emphasize judgement and methodology at the expense of proof and knowledge content. It is also possible, though relatively rare, for a basic unit whose domain of inquiry is unarguably context-dependent to act as if it were not, and so to teach its students as if it were dispensing a body of received doctrine in the process of equipping them to be, in their own right, explorers at the ever-receding frontiers of knowledge. But the parallels and connections we have drawn do, nevertheless, hold good for the majority of basic units located towards one end or other of the positivist—relativist axis.

It remains, having sketched out this particular form of differentiation, to follow up some of its possible consequences and to relate it to the other two value domains discussed earlier in this chapter. We have already indicated some of the distinctions between positivism and relativism in the operational mode. Students in positivistically biased units will usually face a fairly heavy workload, related to the insistence on coverage of large areas of subject-matter, and comparatively frequent assessment tasks. They will tend to develop an atomistic view of knowledge (reality as comprising a multiplicity of nuggets of truth), and their learning styles will usually be syllabus-bound. Those in relativistically biased units will in contrast be likely to enjoy a moderate workload, and their assessment will usually be concentrated at the end of the course (by which time they will be expected to have mastered the necessary techniques of inquiry and developed some sense of judgement). Such students typically acquire a holistic view of knowledge, seeing reality as a constantly changing tissue of interrelated ideas. Unlike their positivistic counterparts, their learning approaches can be characterized as syllabus-free.

As far as staff are concerned, working within a positivistically oriented basic unit serves to create considerable pressure for corporate professional activity. Since advancement is earned in terms of productivity in generating new knowledge, it is necessary to become highly specialized and to keep up a flow of publication. Relationships with students incline towards formality and good teaching resolves itself into the efficient transmission of large quantities of closely defined material. As against this, the pace of life in a relativistically oreinted unit will tend to be easier, with a more informal set of relationships between colleagues and a more varied pattern of commitment to non-teaching activities. Many such units are firmly student-centred, and staff—student relationships are accordingly expected to be open and friendly. Teaching is seen as a transaction whose effectiveness is measured in terms of the extent of active learning.

The relationship between the positivist—relativist axis, the research—technology—scholarship triangle and the closed/permeable cohesive/discrete curricular matrix is not altogether simple and straightforward. Each category can be seen as a different dimension along which the normative characteristics of basic units can be charted. The three together provide a more complex, and perhaps more refined, development of the well-known distinctions between strong and weak classification and framing.[7]

However, the three categories are not independent of one another. It is possible roughly to correlate the research apex of the triangle with the positivist end of the axis (though, as was implied earlier, a research-oriented unit might well take important aspects of its task as interpretative). Similarly, there seems to be a degree of kinship between the scholarship apex and the relativist end of the axis (though again, as already noted, scholarship-oriented units could in some instances insist on hard, quantitative data). The technology/profession apex does not project neatly on to one end or the other, being diffused between the two. Again, within the curriculum matrix, the cohesive—closed cell could be filled by either positivistic or relativistic curricula developed by either research- or scholarship-oriented units. The cohesive—open cell would probably favour relativism and technology/profession; the discrete—closed could most easily accommodate positivism and research; and the discrete—open, relativism and scholarship. But it must be emphasised once again that these equations are only approximate, and allow of numerous exceptions.

The Resilience of Basic Units
We noted earlier in this chapter that basic units tend to differ in terms of their calls on institutional resources, according to whether they are research, technology or scholarship based; and that the curricular patterns which they espouse may have certain implications for the way their parent institution is organized. But more remains to be said about the relationship of basic units to institutions, particularly in respect of attempts on the part of the institution to influence the values or practices of its basic units.

One of the noticeable features of higher education, which our model helps to underline, is the resilience of basic units in the face of institutional pressure of this kind. The observation should not be altogether surprising, since the basic unit has been defined as the smallest viable grouping in any academic institution, working within its own budget and, to a sizeable extent, its own terms of reference. It represents a coherent academic ideology, in a way that larger groupings (say the entire arts faculty) seldom do.[8] It has a key role in the selection of its own members and in determining the curriculum it offers. What is more, the basic unit usually forms part of a wider peer-group network outside the bounds of its parent institution — a network within which individual and collective reputations are established and prospects of mobility and promotion are opened up.

Basic units serve not only as an immediate and direct source of academic identity for individual students and staff, but also as vehicles for the preservation and development of specialist expertise. In this latter respect, they occupy a powerful, though not impregnable, position in the political line-up of the institutions to which they belong. It is not easy for an institution as a whole to call for this or that modification of policy or practice in one of its basic units. In many cases, the unit in question will have the monopoly of relevant specialized knowledge and will be able to respond by rejecting the demand as ill-informed, irrelevant or inappropriate. In a case of conflict it will be more easily able to close its ranks than will the rest of the institution, with its ideologically diverse interest groups. In the last resort, however, the institution can depend on the judgements of those members of staff whose expertise, though different, is closely allied to that of the basic unit in question; or on the views of outside authorities in the same academic field. Where the institution's proposals are upheld, it will have the means of implementing them through its powers to control the unit's budgetary allocations.

Such conflicts between basic units and institutions tend to be confined to cases where the unit has fallen badly out of line both with institutional policy and with contemporary practice in comparable units elsewhere. For the most part, as has been suggested in Chapter 5, the institution is concerned with academic rule-setting and maintenance, with the formulation of a collective response to external demands, with the promotion of promising developments and with a general fiduciary responsibility, rather than with the appraisal of standards of excellence or with the monitoring of the academic norms of its basic units. The senior members of the institution can only directly affect the normative mode when a new head of a basic unit is to be appointed: and even in this instance their scope is limited by the need for approval from the wider specialist peer group outside the institution itself.

The Peer Network and the Market Mechanism

The position of the basic units is given added strength by the underlying continuities of the academic enterprise. They are protected by the appeal to proper processes of inquiry and the need for validated evidence, as against the use of the superior force of systems or institutions. They can trade on the tradition of deferring to expert knowledge, as opposed to using arguments from expediency. But above all, they can depend on a separate structure of values and rewards, based on their particular specialist field, which is national, if not international, in scope.

Every such structure, built up round its own particular set of academic concerns, is of its nature protective of its members' interests and conservative of its corporate practice and reputation. It is rarely amenable to rapid change, and thus provides its constituent basic units with a convenient court of appeal in the face of institutional or central demands for reforms in policy and practice.

The series of 'invisible colleges', as they have been called, which define the networks of specialized interest groups throughout the learned world, are no less powerful for being informal in nature. Each network does, however, incorporate certain formal elements whose purpose is to monitor and safeguard standards. Thus, as we noted in Chapter 4, the systems of academic validation in the UK, based on external examiners (and also, in the case of the maintained sector, on peer-group scrutiny of initial course proposals), can be seen not only as providing public certification but as policing internal practice.

Other visible and formal manifestations of these invisible and informal colleges may include research councils (whose specialist committees are dominated by leading exponents of the relevant discipline), learned societies, and journals which adjudicate acceptability for publication. The offering or withholding of research funds, of membership of prestigious bodies, or of opportunities to publish, is one form of control exercised by the establishment in any given field over the basic units and individuals in that field. Another but less common form of control is provided, in the case of UK universities, by the activities of the specialist subcommittees of the UGC – again composed of distinguished practitioners. It is as a result of their regular scrutiny of the basic units within their field of interest that decisions are made by the main committee about possible areas of growth, or even of potential closure.

Looked at from one point of view, this principle of mutual judgement by specialists of one another's work is inherently fair and sound. It helps to maintain overall standards; at the same time, by providing basic units with an external frame of reference, it ensures that each unit is more than simply the

sum of its individual members. But considered in a less positive light, the powerful position of peer-group networks can
be seen to hold certain dangers. In particular, their strong
protection of established procedures can have an inhibiting
effect on necessary or desirable changes; and the prevailing
orthodoxy, as represented in a few influential figures, can
systematically penalize the basic unit which — perhaps with
good reason — fails to subscribe to the party line. Moreover,
the recommendations of outsiders professing a specialist
interest can sometimes conflict with the views of those concerned to maintain a balanced development within an institution as a whole.

Were it to rely solely on the device of peer networks for
shaping the norms of its basic units, the higher education
system could therefore well become inbred. As it happens,
however, there is an alternative set of considerations which
lies largely outside the system but which powerfully affects
the way in which it behaves. We referred in Chapter 2 to the
social and economic climate as providing an important contextual element to our model: at this point, we can see it
directly in operation.

The alternative currency to that of academic prestige, as
far as basic units are concerned, is the marketability of
courses. Although the two are by no means unconnected,
they have somewhat independent effects. Thus, for example,
although the standing of management studies is not particularly high in the pecking order of learned pursuits, the
basic units which provide degree courses in it may gain a
certain measure of esteem within their institutions by virtue
of the fact that their courses are usually oversubscribed. In a
similar way, despite the high scholarly status traditionally
granted to the study of Latin and Greek, the absence of any
substantial student demand for places in classics departments inevitably affects their power and their credibility
inside their parent universities.

The student numbers game — the tailoring of teaching
programmes to suit the potential customer — can be thought
of as a necessary antidote to the otherwise excessive intro-
spection of peer-group monitoring. It is certainly, as we shall
see in Chapter 9, a major source of innovative ideas in teaching, learning and curricular design. But it cannot be played

with complete disregard for the views of the peer network, any more than the leading members of that network can afford to ignore the influence of market forces. The two currencies are not, as we have already observed, mutually independent. If a basic unit goes in too blatantly for attracting students, at the expense of upholding disciplinary traditions, it risks being cut off from membership of its invisible college, and hence from offering a recognized academic qualification; this immediately and drastically reduces the marketability of its courses. Equally, an effective specialist guild or network must be alive to happenings in the schools, in the field of graduate employment and, more generally, in current intellectual fashion. In the effort to defend and improve its standing in society, it has to be ready to take action in its constituents' interests as one political pressure group among many others, without at the same time losing its distinctive academic role.

We shall subsequently return to consider some of these points in more detail. For the present, it remains to be noted that we have said relatively little about the relationships between basic units and the individuals, whether staff or students, who belong to them. This is a sufficiently important element of our model to deserve separate examination, and we shall therefore take it up in the next chapter.

7. The Individual Level

Staff and Basic Units

In terms of our initial model, it is possible to consider both students and staff from two aspects — normative and operational — although, as with all other levels of the system, the aspects are closely interconnected (Figure 7.1).

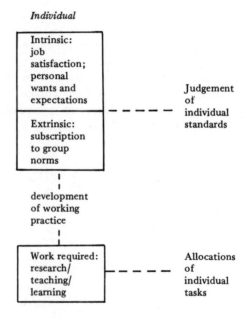

Figure 7.1 Functions of the individual

The discussion of basic units has already given some pointers to the predominant values of academic staff. The most useful starting point is, perhaps, a recognition that the main currency for the academic is not power (as it is for the politician) nor wealth (as it is for the businessman), but reputation. To be held in good esteem by one's colleagues, to earn the intellectual admiration of one's students, to become somebody of consequence in one's subject field — these will tend to be high among the initial hopes of anyone embarking on an academic career. Much, then, of the driving force behind what academics do is concerned with building up, or maintaining, a professional reputation.[1]

To say so is not to deny that teaching staff can have other motivations, or that they might decide at some point in their careers to abandon their initial concern in favour of another, quite different one. It is only to underline the fact that the climate of values within which academics are nurtured, and which they are subsequently expected to sustain, strongly favours the pursuit of a good name in one's particular trade. This in its turn calls for both a creative contribution to a particular field of inquiry and identification with the interests of colleagues engaged in the same activity.

The ingredients of a good reputation vary from subject area to subject area and basic unit to basic unit. Disciplines which are strongly research-oriented call for a different set of skills from subjects which stress the virtues of scholarship; and both are different again from those concerned with a technology or a profession. Moreover, as we have noted in Chapter 6, basic units whose underlying approach is positivistic place different demands on their members from those which favour a relativistic stance.

When allowance is made for the differences in the way an academic reputation can be earned, the unifying characteristic remains one of a strong identification with a discipline, coupled with a concern to preserve and enhance its public reputation as much as one's own private one. The major, but relatively rare, exception to this rule is when a group from a particular academic pursuit manages successfully to establish an independent and hitherto undeveloped field of inquiry — as, for example, in the hiving off of radio astronomers from their parent departments in a number of universities in the 1950s and 1960s. In such a case the process is not unlike the resignation of members of a club whose interests have too much diverged from those of the majority of their fellows, leading to the subsequent founding of a rival group. Nor is it altogether different from the secession of a disaffected colony or border territory, leading to the establishment of an independent state.[2]

The possibility of secession itself serves to underline the element of ideology behind the practice of a discipline. It sometimes seems almost as if the inherent logic of inquiry, and the lines which it opens up for further exploration, have an independent existence which can somehow control the destinies of those who pursue it. There are cases where whole career patterns have altered, creating sizeable problems of de-skilling. One might describe this unquestioning acceptance of the direction of intellectual evolution as the academic counterpart of 'my country, right or wrong'.

Looked at from another perspective, intrinsic ideology can operate alongside extrinsic manipulation. Disciplines are notoriously subject to fashion. It is those practitioners who are most closely in tune with current trends who hold the main political leadership within the discipline. It would be disingenuous to think that such people do not strive to create new fashions in a direction which further enhances their own prestige.

The argument begins at this point to take the familiar shape of a dispute between the realists and the nominalists: those who wish to maintain that academic knowledge is somehow 'out there' for the finding, and those who suggest that it is no more than a social construct.[3] The dispute predates Plato and Aristotle and is unlikely to lend itself to brief settlement here. We simply remark that there are occasions when a major breakthrough in understanding transcends all attempts, even by the most strongly established interests, to confine it within the existing barricades of power.[4]

In any event, as far as the issue of disciplinary identity is concerned, there is a fairly clear correlation between intellectual proximity to the existing centres of interest and general academic reputation. The descent is steepest in the more hierarchical subjects. For example, a chemist employed in the pathology department of a medical school (and hence not even a 'proper chemist' any longer, however good the quality of his or her work) has to fight very hard to maintain membership of, and status within, the orthodox professional community. Within more democratic and collegial disciplines, the slope of the decline is more gradual between reputation and marginality of status. Thus someone specializing in contemporary West African literature or researching into Welsh local history, though manifestly not among those most professionally or publicly visible, would scarcely be disbarred from disciplinary membership as a literature specialist or historian.

The most obvious exception to this general link between orthodoxy and status is provided by the highly inventive academic who works outside the prevailing conventions of his discipline. In effect, he must be prepared to take a major gamble with his reputation, staking it on the possibility of creating a new centre of influence. On rare occasions — as in the cases of Einstein or F. R. Leavis — the gamble comes off. But if it does, one begins to describe the situation as an example of polycentrism rather than marginality, so preserving the integrity of the original claim.

The Obligation to Teach
The academic's occupational quest for reputation, in the sense so far discussed, is complicated by an accompanying activity which at present has little to do with it. When reviewing the recruitment criteria, incentives, rewards and group values which form the main relationships between individuals and basic units at the normative levels, it is easy to overlook the fact that, in operational terms, the academic staff of institutions of higher education are primarily employed to teach. To point the paradox, tenured teachers are recruited largely on their records and potential for research, which is also the main activity by which they are judged for promotion.[5] The premium placed on research is clearly marked in the UK by the status difference between the reader (a highly regarded research-based appointment) and the — equally paid — senior lecturer (a reward for faithful service, commanding respect rather than admiration).

It is too much to say that teaching provides no pay-offs other than in a monetary sense. Some academics find their teaching duties intrinsically satisfying and rewarding, and accept their obligations to students with willingness, if not enthusiasm. And some institutions — not only those which do not emphasize the traditions of research, technology and scholarship (and where, therefore, staff have little to do but teach) — put a premium on excellence in curriculum planning and in classroom communication. Nevertheless, considering the central part that it plays in the operational aspects of academic institutions, and the extent to which the funding of those institutions is justified in terms of the numbers of students they attract, the teaching function of the individual member of staff remains oddly undervalued.[6]

There seem to be two main reasons for this state of affairs. The first has already been indirectly considered. We have noted that subject loyalties within academia tend to be extremely strong, and that the academic's related concern with reputation is focused on the fulfilment of the expectation that one should contribute to and promote one's chosen discipline. The leading practitioners — namely, those who set the standards which others seek to follow — usually reach their leading positions because of the energies which they put into earning a reputation in these terms. Not surprisingly, few of them have a similar degree of creative energy to spare for undergraduate teaching, and thus they do not portray it as an activity of anything like comparable significance. The influential members of the peer group, in other words, give no strong lead in the direction of regarding teaching as a serious intellectual task.

The second reason relates to the institutional conditions under which teaching activities normally take place. By long tradition (broken only by the occasional co-operative venture in course development or team teaching), the quality of the interaction between a member of staff and his or her students is regarded as an essentially personal matter. Teaching problems are not a generally accepted topic of discussion among colleagues, and the practicalities of giving lectures or tutorials, or running seminars or laboratory classes, have not until very recently been thought to need any explicit preparation. Like sex among the British, teaching has remained in the realm of the private, the unspoken and the amateur. So competence as a teacher is not easily assessed, especially in contrast with research (or consultancy, or scholarship) whose processes are often visible to colleagues and whose products are usually within the public domain.

There is, accordingly, no commonly established means by which individual excellence in devising a course, in putting across ideas or in helping students to explore ideas of their own can be identified – and hence no mechanism by which such competence can be rewarded. Even though it might be thought that ways round this difficulty could and should be devised, so far few institutions seem to have done so successfully.[7] That may say something about institutional priorities as between the earning of academic reputations and the provision of high-quality teaching programmes. In any event, the outcome is that there is no extrinsic reward for putting major efforts into the improvement of teaching: so that while those who enjoy it will continue to earn their intrinsic sense of satisfaction from a job well done, the majority of their colleagues will tend not to see it as a matter of prime importance. This view, as we shall see, has inevitable consequences for the students' perspective on their academic experience and on their relationships with the basic unit to which they belong.

The Full-Time Researcher

There is a small subgroup of academic staff who escape any conflict of priorities between teaching and research, by virtue of the fact that they are employed as full-time researchers. The differences between staff in this category and their colleagues who have been appointed as teachers are numerous, and serve to underline some of the major adjustments which would need to be made to the model in Chapter 2 if it were to relate specifically to the research component in higher education.

In the first place, the large majority of research-based appointments are temporary. Their incumbents do not enjoy the same privileges of tenure as teaching staff, and are usually on short-term contracts. Individuals may continue to work on this basis, as part of a kind of itinerant labour force, for substantial periods – though in the end most appear to succumb to the growing pressures on them to take up some permanent post (whether inside academia, in some independent research body, in industry or in the public services). As temporary inhabitants of any particular academic scene, they enjoy few of the privileges of staff membership. In particular, they seldom achieve any foothold within the political structure of their institution — nor are they likely to be entrusted with, or burdened by, administrative responsibilities outside their own research units.

Second, while tenured academics have — at least in theory — a free range of choice over their research topics, professional researchers are explicitly contracted to work on a defined project under the authority of a named research director. They may choose whether or not to apply for a given job, but once appointed they forfeit most of the discretion that their teaching-based counterparts take for granted. Pursuing this distinction further, a member of teaching staff works largely within a collegial relationship in his or her basic unit, even if one which is ultimately dependent on the head of the unit for resources, operational tasks and recommendations for promotion. In contrast, the relationship of a director of research with a member of the team on contract is virtually that of a manager to a subordinate, no matter what the style of work may be. In the central structure of the academic institution, accountability is blurred. In a research unit it is quite clear: the director is professionally accountable to the funding agency (usually outside the institution, and even outside the central authorities responsible for higher education); the contracted staff are in their turn accountable for all their work to the director.

The role of the research unit's director underlines some of these distinctions. Almost invariably, he is part of the institutional establishment — a tenured academic, more often than not running the research part-time (though in a few cases he may occupy a post fully endowed for research, or be given a special appointment in his own right which frees him of all other commitments). As a head of department, such an individual would have to negotiate staffing resources, annual budgets and physical facilities in close competition with other departmental heads. In no circumstances could he by-pass the institutional level to approach the central authorities directly. But as director (or potential director) of a research unit, he would enjoy far fewer constraints. In negotiating with an outside grant-giving body, he need only secure administrative confirmation (as opposed to academic agreement) that the institution would administer any grant, and perhaps contribute accommodation and other facilities in kind. With this done, he would have a more or less free hand to approach any appropriate funding agency and to contract to carry out any reasonable research programme (except one with classified subject-matter, which would require institutional approval).

This distinction between the relative freedom of setting up research programmes and the careful institutional safeguards which surround proposals for new teaching schemes points up an interesting paradox — and one which is compounded by the marginal status of research units and full-time research staff. The common observation that, in most institutions of higher education, research enjoys greater prestige than teaching seems to be falsified by a closer examination of funded projects and their comparatively weak integration within the institutional structure.[8]

The explanation which suggests itself for this contradictory state of affairs depends on the distinction drawn in our model in Chapter 2 between the normative and the operational modes. It is clear that, normatively, both the individual academic and the basic unit are prone to regard research as a primary activity and teaching only as a secondary one; even at the level of the institution and the central authorities, its significance is far from negligible. But operationally, research is heavily parasitic on the teaching programme. Money, manpower and materials are determined largely by student numbers: identifiably separate funds for research form a minor part of the overall pattern of resources, and so command very little interest, whether at the institutional or the basic unit level. Individual attitudes are shaped accordingly: tenured teaching staff are aware that, operationally, they owe their post first and foremost to teaching; untenured research staff must often feel themselves, in operational terms, to be defined by their conditions of service as second-class citizens.

The Academic and the Outside World

We have argued that the traditions of British higher education encourage individual academics to act, in terms of their professional identity, in a highly entrepreneurial way. Where most other social institutions require their members to adopt convergent values and practices, universities — and, to a growing extent, polytechnics and colleges — put a premium on creative divergence. Individual distinction, competitively assessed, in research or consultancy or scholarship is held to strengthen the reputation of the basic unit which has housed and sponsored the work, and more remotely that of the institution which has provided resources for it.

There are, however, certain quite powerful, if indirect, constraints on individual autonomy. Even within the basic unit itself, teaching, though commonly regarded as a personal matter with regard to style and approach, has to some extent to be co-ordinated in terms of content within a given course, and to an even more obvious extent in terms of time and space. The advancement of learning — as opposed to its promotion in others — will often involve collaborative work of some kind, in which the need to maintain a commonality of purpose and a sensible division of labour limits the freedom of action of individual team members.

Within academia at large, there are institutional constraints and peer-group norms which operate in ways we have already discussed. But outside pressures — less predictable, less amenable to direct influence and hence somehow more inexorable — also condition what the individual academic is able to do. In the wider environment in which the system is accommodated, the disposition of market forces at any given time can enhance or limit the opportunities for pursuing a reputation in one field or another. ·

The impact of these market forces is in two main directions. The first affects some — but not all — disciplinary areas: namely, those in which academic work at the individual or basic unit level is to some degree dependent on the support of public bodies or private benefactors. Such funding agencies may have their own budgets suddenly reduced by a sharp decline in economic growth; or they may decide, for one reason or another, to develop new policy initiatives outside the area in question. The net result in either case is likely to be a reduction in the level of active large-scale research or development.

The second direction of impact is indiscriminate in its

effects, and is liable to affect any and every subject field: namely, the ability of basic units to recruit students. Here the vagaries of the economy may be reinforced by the remorseless inevitability of the birth rate to produce a situation demanding quite drastic structural change.[9] Paradoxically, the individuals in a discipline which is much in demand may find themselves with heavy teaching commitments and relatively little time for advancing their own professional careers, though the necessary supporting resources may be more than adequate; those in a subject whose lack of student numbers allows them ample time to pursue their own academic interests may be hindered from doing so through lack of funds and facilities. (Good institutional management may equalize the balance over time, but such adjustment is necessarily slow in a time of retrenchment.)

These external pressures are themselves part of the setting within which the central authorities make decisions. The responses which they make may be both material and symbolic, leading not only to changes in allocations of resources but also to status rewards and appointments which favour leading individuals and so signal strong support for a particular field of activity. Governmental patronage may thus provide a direct and immediate link between the contemporary social climate and a limited number of leading academics.

It is, however, important to recall the argument in Chapter 3 that the academic peer system is co-opted by the central authorities into both the normative and operational modes, and that this serves to protect basic units and individuals against purely administrative decisions. There has in effect to be an accommodation between the academic ambitions of individuals on the one hand and the demands for qualified manpower and for efficient management by central authorities on the other. We return to the point that every academic is expected to exercise his own sense of integrity, even when working in collaboration with other colleagues: the limitations on him are not those of command from higher authority, but of negotiation between his saleable expertise and the supporting facilities and resources afforded by the state.

Changes in the external environment can thus be seen to impinge in a variety of ways on individual academics.

They may give rise to normative shifts in the central authorities, which are then operationalized by adjusting the pattern of resource allocations to institutions, and (less directly) basic units and individuals. These operational changes may in due course lead individuals to modify their own norms, and collectively to adjust the norms of the basic unit. But new economic and social pressures can also impinge directly on academics as members of the wider society, and cause them to change their own sense of priorities. The values of academics, viewed in this wider context, are clearly not as self-contained as some of the protagonists — or some of the detractors — of the doctrine of academic freedom are inclined to suggest.

Students and their Studies

At this point we turn to another important but surprisingly often neglected group of individuals within the higher education system. It is not easy to generalize about the characteristics of students in UK universities, polytechnics and colleges, particularly as, at the undergraduate level, the pattern is no longer a relatively uniform one of 18-year-old English school-leavers, the large majority coming from middle-class home backgrounds. But even though students may be of differing ages, nationalities and (to a lesser extent) social backgrounds, there are nevertheless certain fairly constant features of their behaviour, and there is a certain predictability about their attitudes, which it may be useful to examine in the context of our model.

In the first place, various psychologists have suggested that learning styles can be located along a number of closely related continua. Thus Bruner refers to a 'focusing/scanning' antithesis; Hudson to 'convergence' and 'divergence'; Marton to 'something that happens to you' versus 'something you do'; Pask to 'serialist' and 'holist' strategies.[10] One might, at some risk of oversimplification, relate these categories to common-sense notions of active and passive learning. A passive approach suggests treating pieces of knowledge as separate entities to be acquired in a serial fashion; an active approach implies synthesis, the bringing together of apparently distinct pieces of information so as to develop some sort of structure or pattern.

There is a temptation to ask if there could be some connection between the value contrasts implicit in this spectrum of learning styles and the differing ideologies behind the positivistic/relativistic approaches discussed in Chapter 6 above. It is debatable whether one can legitimately go further, to suggest that passive learners are attracted by the hierarchical, content-centred curricula of positivistic units, while active learners prefer the more democratic, method-centred curricula which tend to characterize relativistic units. The converse could equally well be argued, that a long dose of positivism in school courses leads to a passive learning style which carries over into higher education, while relativism breeds a disposition to high activity. But in either event, the outcome would appear to be that positivistic units tend to have a high population of passive learners who are intellectually dependent on external authority, and who are more comfortable with the certainty of proof than with the challenge of judgement; while in relativistic units, the opposite pattern obtains.

A second fairly constant feature of the student estate is the basic currency in terms of which most academic activities are evaluated and most future plans assessed. Just as academic staff are guided, as we noted earlier, by the wish to maintain and enhance their scholarly reputations, so students understandably seek to optimize their credit in their final degree assessment. The personal, as well as the occupational sanctions of failure are usually perceived as severe, and this reinforces the students' sense of anxiety to 'make the grade'. Much of this anxiety focuses on the assessment system, and especially on attempts to unravel its complexities, understand its processes and identify the relative weightings of the different components.[11]

One interesting study of the phenomenon of assessment[12] suggests that students fall into three groups. The first, labelled 'cue seekers', quite deliberately set themselves to find out as much as possible (by picking up hints in lectures, asking staff leading questions, scanning previous examination papers, and so on) about their assessment tasks. The second, designated as 'cue conscious', do not themselves take active steps to glean such information but are sensitive to any hints that may be dropped. The third, referred to as 'cue deaf', consider everything that they are taught to be of uniform importance, and set themselves to be assessed on all of it. In the study in question, there was a close correlation between the cue seekers and those awarded first class degrees, the cue conscious and those who got seconds, and the cue deaf and those who got thirds or worse.

The students' concern with 'earning marks' is often deplored by staff — much as the leisured classes used from time to time to bemoan the obsession of the lower orders with being paid for what they did, rather than offering to do it voluntarily. The divergence of value on this point can, if it becomes pronounced, give rise to problems. A frequent cause of contention is the confidentiality of marks and of examination board discussions. The main fear by staff is that too much knowledge of what happens could lead to unjustified but damaging litigation by disappointed candidates. The common concern of students is that apparently arbitrary and unfair decisions might remain unchallenged.

As we shall note in Chapter 8, student discontent about assessment procedures has in the past led to substantial reforms in the examination system. At a more trivial level, the insistence of staff on keeping even purely procedural information confidential, to discourage students from 'playing the numbers game', seldom succeeds in its object. The espionage system may be good or bad: either way a folklore soon builds up. If it is indeed based on fallacious premises, the students are merely penalized by misdirecting their energies in a way that has nothing to do with academic merit.

A third identifiable characteristic of most students' careers seems to be a sequential change of attitudes, abilities and anxieties over time. Perhaps understandably, in the early stages of their courses in higher education, students are beset by a good deal of uncertainty over norms and expectations. They find it difficult to establish, for example, what is considered in their particular field to be a reasonable amount of work for a week; how long their essays should be; how many set exercises they should tackle; what standard of performance is viewed by staff as reasonable for a first-year student; and so on. They are also liable to sense a certain amount of confusion about the nature and identity of their subject field. A characteristic pattern in the middle stages of the course is that, with these questions resolved, students experience a falling-off in enthusiasm and develop a perception of their work as being somewhat routine-bound. Their heavy initial dependence on staff can in some cases be overcompensated by a deliberate distancing as they attempt to establish their own independence and identity. But it is usually not until the final stages of the undergraduate course — and sometimes not until after it has ended — that students acquire some sense of mastery of their subject field, a confidence in their own abilities to understand its underlying methods and principles, and a full sense of autonomy as people who can guide their own learning.[13]

Students as Social Beings
Some general features can be noted of students' relationships with one another. The milieu in which they work tends to be one of competition rather than co-operation (certain basic units strive to counteract this in the structure of their undergraduate programmes, but even in their case, the classified degree system imposes strong competitive strains). As a result, the operational pattern of students' work is in general individualistic: corporate activities are rare, and in many instances (helping friends with, or asking friends' help on, assignments) are discouraged. In this competitive atmosphere, students commonly admit to a reluctance to seem foolish in front of their peers: and this leads to their hesitating to ask staff for clarification of points they have failed to understand. The consequence can be a situation in which large numbers of students are floundering, while each of them thinks all the others have managed to keep their heads above water, and their teacher assumes that none at all is out of his or her depth.[14]

Particular problems can arise in courses with a significant proportion of atypical students — for example, those from overseas or those entering at a mature age, often with unorthodox qualifications. Overseas undergraduates, depending on their country or origin, may suffer from linguistic handicaps and from the difficulties of adjustment to an unfamiliar culture and an alien educational tradition. Their presence in a group is sometimes resented as slowing down the pace of learning and as calling for a disproportionate share of tutorial attention. Mature students present a different set of difficulties. They tend to be considerably more anxious than recent school-leavers about their academic performance and potentiality, and are liable to take up substantial amounts of staff time in seeking reassurance that they are doing what is required of them. As against this, they are usually more confident in social terms than most students straight from school, and their easy relationships with academics can also cause resentment. So can their attitudes to younger members of the course, which are often perceived as patronizing[15] . The internal tensions which result within heterogeneous student groups of this kind are seldom serious enough to come into the open, but it does not follow that they have a negligible effect on the quality of learning.

Within the system as a whole, relations between students and staff can and do vary enormously. However, the structure of academic institutions provides an inbuilt tendency towards an 'us and them' division: a discernible psychological barrier between teachers and taught. One inquiry has portrayed this in terms of a metaphor of Victoran rural England, with staff as gentry and students as villagers:

> By and large the gentry and villagers regard themselves as moving in different spheres, although they interact in common work pursuits where role and status differences are closely marked out. If they meet outside this context, in non-work settings, they feel less comfortable — how to relate appropriately is not laid down, and there are taboos on both sides against 'breaking rank'. (It is not uncommon in some institutions for staff who spend time with students, or invite them to their homes, to be regarded as somehow 'odd' by colleagues.) Overwhelmingly, despite the uprisings of the late sixties, the villagers still relate to the gentry with deference; they are pleased when they are noticed and despondent when criticized. As they get older and status increases (in their final year) they may get closer to the gentry, are known and taken into confidence more, and may even reach first name terms. But for many, throughout their time in higher education, a distance prevails.[16]

The divide between students and their teachers is to some extent built into the basic educational contract between someone who has knowledge and someone who does not. Assessment is another obvious factor in promoting social distance. Other incidental ones may include differences in age, income, occupational status and leisure interests. However, given that some sort of barrier is probably unavoidable, its height and solidity can be adjusted by changes in the ethos of basic units and the attitudes of individuals within them.

There is a good deal of evidence to suggest that the context in which students learn — the range of their relationships with the basic unit in whose programmes they are engaged — can have a direct effect on their efficiency as learners. In those situations in which the atmosphere is formal and impersonal, students comment (not perhaps surprisingly) that they feel alienated and inhibited. In those which encourage a direct and personal contact between teachers and taught, they feel more easily able to ask for help over their difficulties. What has been called 'the hidden curriculum' can have an impact on a student's learning experience which is none the less powerful for remaining inexplicit and unexamined.[17]

There is also a somewhat less direct link between staff—student relationships and the quality of teaching. In any given course, the teacher will have certain conscious or unconscious expectations about connections which will be made, analogies which will be understood, crucial points which will be noted by those he or she teaches. In nearly all cases where a member of staff decides at the end of the course to put such assumptions directly to the test by questioning students about how the message came across, or how the intentions worked out in practice, he or she will admit to having made a number of surprising discoveries. The finding that some particular aspect of the teaching has not worked as it was intended to will usually lead to some attempt to put it right — and so, with any luck, to a positive improvement when the course is next given. But where the divide between staff and students is too wide to allow for the kind of honest reporting which such exercises demand, the teachers in question are denied at least one important means of checking that their courses are being interpreted in the way they expect. The likelihood is that, over time, they will build up a good many erroneous assumptions about what can be taken as learned, and that their students will become progressively more alienated and confused.

Students' unions are increasingly involved in the relationship of students to staff, and students to other students. First, they offer a social base, as well as counselling and recreational facilities, sometimes in competition with basic units or with the institution as a whole. Within the union itself, the characteristics of student individualism to which we have already referred are maintained — so that, for example, elections for office can be fiercely fought no matter how much solidarity may be created on particular issues.

Those who take an active part in student union affairs become members of a reward system not dependent on staff evaluations. Student leaders have access to property, funds and power; regardless of academic performance, they may become leading campus personalities with whom negotiations must be conducted. The unions thus have their own patterns of deference, dependency and resource allocation in those institutions where they have achieved full political viability.

Postscript on Postgraduates

We have not attempted a complete inventory of those who play a part in the lives of academic institutions. Administrative and ancillary staff, for example, exercise a vital role in underpinning the operational activities of any university, polytechnic or college, but since they serve no significant function in determining its norms they are of little direct relevance to our analysis. Postgraduates are another group who, although they apparently enjoy at least the limited participatory rights of students, are marginal to the enterprise in much the way that we have observed full-time contract researchers to be. There is a distinction to be made here between students on taught master's degree courses, who are often treated as if they were more mature undergraduates, and those on doctoral programmes.

With a few notable exceptions (Cambridge, for example, has a Graduate Centre offering the amenities of a first-rate club, and several recently established graduate colleges), the institutional provision for doctoral students is much more limited than that for undergraduates. On the arts and social science side, such students may complain of a sense of isolation, since their academic contact with the institution is largely confined to a single supervisor (who, because often a senior academic, may prove very difficult to track down). On the science and technology side, far from being isolated doctoral students are often herded into an overcrowded laboratory, and entrusted with intellectually menial tasks, whose purpose they may fail to understand but whose completion promises them the doctoral reward they seek. Both categories of student are offered limited teaching assignments (for example, as tutors to first-year undergraduates or as laboratory demonstrators), but are rarely given initial help on how to teach.

This state of affairs is a relic from the time when the proportion of postgraduates in the total student population was small, and any special arrangements would arguably have been uneconomic. However, in many universities (less so in public sector institutions) this proportion has risen steadily to 20 per cent or more: so it is on the face of it puzzling that the postgraduate's marginal status remains virtually unchanged. Two explanations suggest themselves, the one couched in anthropological terms and the other in political. First, it can be suggested, the institution sees its doctoral postgraduates — and indeed they see themselves — as initiates to academia. So it is understandable that a rite of passage should be devised — in the doctoral dissertation — which is deliberately given the features of an ordeal. To make things too easy would be to fail to put disciplinary devotion to a proper test. Second, the contrived physical and intellectual isolation of those students who are most likely to be politically active — the social scientists and those working in the humanities — renders them ineffective as a pressure group; in contrast, the norms of the scientists require them to accept hierarchical authority, and not to reason why, so their continual presence on campus does not constitute much of a threat. Since, as was suggested in Chapter 5, academic institutions share many of the characteristics of political systems, it is understandable that underdogs who neither bark nor bite are — albeit unconsciously — treated as if they were dumb and toothless.

8. Initiating and Adapting to Change

The Process of Innovation

This chapter and its successor mark a shift of emphasis from the four which have preceded it. Chapters 4 to 7 have been concerned with exploring the characteristic norms and operations of each level of the system in turn. Chapters 8 and 9, in contrast, aim respectively to characterize the relationships between one mode and another and one level and another. The difference in purpose necessarily brings with it a change of both content and style. The argument becomes illustrative rather than analytic; the complex of interconnections between components in the model is less firmly delineated than the components themselves have been; more emphasis is given to particular instances of general processes.

It was suggested in Chapter 2 that the links between the normative and the operational modes should be taken to represent a state of dynamic equilibrium. A predisposition for change is created when the normative and operational elements at any level become significantly out of phase. The situation will usually give rise to some appropriate change in belief or practice designed to restore normal functioning. Once the necessary degree of congruence has been re-established, the system reverts to equilibrium once more.

It is important to be clear about the nature and limits of this analysis. The validity of the metaphor which it embodies remains to be established, and we shall take that to be one of our tasks in the discussion which follows. For the present, it should be emphasized that the notation we have adopted to account for innovation in the higher education system is certainly not intended to imply that the origins of change are always parochial. On the contrary, as we shall go on to illustrate, innovative pressures may derive from the wider social environment, or from the peer group at large, as well as from higher or from lower levels within the system itself. But while the *origins* can be widespread, the actual *process* of innovation is, we would claim, localized and specific. Chapter 4 has argued that we are not dealing with a hierarchical system, where change can be decreed from above, but rather with a negotiative one, in which individuals, basic units and institutions each regard themselves as having the right to decide what is best for them. It follows that any innovative proposal has to be finally sanctioned by those who are in a position to put it into effect. We have chosen to underline this characteristic of the system by locating the innovation process at a specific level — whichever one is appropriate to the case — and by identifying it as a mediation at that level between norms and operations, one or other of which has been affected by extrinsic considerations.

This abstract account of the process of change in higher education may usefully be tested against other analyses of innovation. The literature on innovation theory is sizeable. Some studies are very general, attempting to account for any change in any kind of institutional setting; others are specific, confining themselves to institutions of a particular type. One of the most influential writers has been Kurt Lewin, whose 'field theory'[1] has a wide frame of reference. The depiction of change in our model, though not as detailed as Lewin's, is clearly consistent with it. It is even more closely compatible with a recent study of curriculum innovation in Swedish universities, based on seven detailed and closely documented case-studies.[2] Although the terminology used by the authors differs from our own (being closely based on Lewin's notions of 'cracks', 'unfreezing', 'driving and restraining forces' and 're-freezing'), the sequence of ideas and the structure of the argument are more or less identical.

It is one thing to argue that the model we have put forward, in so far as it incorporates the concept of innovation, is consistent with at least some theoretical writings on the subject: it is quite another to show that it matches reality. Our next step must be to explore how far our notation is able to accommodate to actual changes which have taken place, or innovations which have proved unsuccessful, at various levels in the system.

Changes to the System as a Whole

The central authorities in any higher education system have an unenviable task. It is their extrinsic function to ensure that the system as a whole appears adequately to meet the needs of society and the economy, and their intrinsic obligation to ensure that proper institutional standards are maintained. Yet in carrying out the extrinsic task, they have no direct way of influencing the activities of the basic units, who are not readily persuaded to abandon their strongly established professional loyalties in favour of demands from above. In meeting the intrinsic requirement (the maintenance of institutional standards) their only obvious form of reward and punishment is through the use of their power to allocate resources. However, a large part of the budgetary total is taken up with continuing commitments, such as staff salaries and basic running costs, which can only be varied gradually over a period of years: and this restrains the ability of the central authorities to generate rapid change without a significant increase in expenditure.

Accordingly, there is no easy way for central authorities to attempt to correct an imbalance between their normative and operational modes — that is to say, when resource commitments and the pattern of course provision move out of line with national policy, however defined. One common strategy is some measure of structural reform, so designed as to affect the pattern of institutional power and to promote activities seen as more educationally desirable or more economically worthwhile than those which already exist.

We shall here briefly examine four of the main recent changes in the category of structural reform in British higher education, and consider with the wisdom of hindsight the degree to which they might be regarded as successful. The first case in point is the establishment of the new universities, as part of the wave of expansion heralded by the Robbins Report in the early 1960s. One of the hopes behind the creation of new institutions, as opposed to the further enlargement of existing ones, was that they would provide a better opportunity for trying out new educational ideas. The initial claims of those who founded them were ambitious: one much-quoted phrase referred to 'drawing a new map of learning'.[3]

In retrospect, it would be fair to claim that the new universities succeeded in introducing certain modifications to the existing maps without significantly altering the landscape. A number of them made genuine attempts to break out of the straitjacket of established academic disciplines. It was only when the staff they recruited began applying for posts in more conventional universities that the real problem was laid bare. Given the choice between a historian and a member of a school of European studies, most history departments will go for the former. However sound the latter's credentials in history might be, his membership of the club is questionable and his loyalty must inevitably be suspect. So until a sufficient number of universities have their own posts in European studies, there will be an inevitable tendency for academics to reassert their original disciplinary identities. An underground network of departments based on traditional subjects is already discernible in most of the institutions dedicated to interdisciplinary teaching and research. A change in a system of currency cannot be brought about unilaterally by a minority group — and that is in part what the new universities were expected to do.

The second example is also related to the expansion of degree-level teaching. In this case, rather than extending the range of university-based provision, the attempt was to provide an alternative to it. (A fuller account is given in Chapter 3.) The creation of a separate, rival sector of higher education (and the laying down of an imaginary boundary — the binary line — to protect it from falling into the academic trap of the universities) took place even before the last of the new universities, Ulster, had been given its charter. New institutions within the maintained sector, designated as polytechnics, were developed from those technical colleges which had an established record of advanced work. Their remit — first spelled out in a speech by the late Anthony Crosland at Woolwich in 1965 — was to concentrate on teaching largely to the exclusion of research, to emphasize vocationally relevant degree programmes, to provide social mobility for students (which might be taken to imply the acceptance of larger numbers of working-class applicants) and to be 'directly responsive to social needs', especially in relation to the local setting.

In the event, none of these ambitions has been fully realized. The basic units in the polytechnics, no less than those in the universities, respond to peer-group norms associated with their disciplines. Their academic staff by and large look outside the institutional structure for their professional identity. Since academic reputation rests on published papers, the opportunity to do research and to conduct scholarly inquiry is claimed as a right. Vocational relevance is not discouraged in degree programmes, but the differences in this respect from university provision are moderate.[4] As for achieving a higher intake of working-class students, the polytechnics are as much in competition for the best-qualified applicants as are the universities. This has meant that they have not in the event recruited a significantly larger proportion of those from working-class backgrounds than the universities have succeeded in doing.[5]

For the same reason, their catchment is national rather than local: they seek to attract students from all parts of the country. Their local ties are therefore relatively weak (except in an adventitious sense, in that their management remains largely in the hands of the local authorities, and most of them recruit a high proportion of part-time students who are necessarily based within commuting distance). This, again, seems a case in which the original intentions of central authority have been powerless when set against the resilience of values in the basic units.[6] In a situation where institutional prestige is highly competitive, it would appear curiously naive to set up a separate and rival system and pronounce it to be 'equal but different'. Only a decade after the polytechnics came into existence, some were openly aspiring to university status: the rest, perhaps more hesitant at abandoning the very principles on which they were founded, none the less seemed anxious to divest themselves of local control and to devise some alternative formula for becoming 'equal and similar'.

The third case of structural reform is of another new institution created to meet socially and politically important needs which remained unsatisfied under existing arrangements. The Open University was given a task which was not directly competitive with that of any existing universities and polytechnics. It was set up to provide degree courses on a part-time basis to mature students working at home, by means of a combination of correspondence tuition, supplementary material broadcast on radio and television, and optional attendance at 'study centres' for face-to-face teaching and counselling. Perhaps partly because it was not seen as posing a direct challenge to other degree-giving institutions, and partly because its key staffing appointments were carefully made to ensure academic acceptability, the Open University quite rapidly came to be regarded as a reputable institution.

Even so, it might have been considered as peripheral to the higher education system as a whole, and as pursuing a worthy but unglamorous task, had it not been for two particular features of its activities. The first was the development of a system of teamwork in the preparation of teaching materials. Because the Open University's teaching is of necessity public rather than private, relying largely on written and broadcast material, the conventional taboo on discussing teaching problems had to be broken. The resulting notion of course teams[7] has had a powerful effect in developing more sophisticated procedures for collective curriculum planning in polytechnics and universities in general. The second feature, closely related to this, is that the Open University's course materials generally achieve a high standard of content and presentation. Because they are all available in published form, they have to meet the kind of scrutiny normally reserved for basic texts; and for the most part they have been judged successfully to pass the test — so much so, indeed, that many OU booklets have become unofficial sources of reference for students in other institutions, if not officially prescribed or recommended course materials.

This particular instance of a structural change has not therefore been beset by the kinds of problem which attended the growth of the new universities or the emergence of the polytechnics. We shall come back to consider the reasons in more detail in the concluding section of this chapter: though as we have already remarked, there is an important difference in the extent to which competition is offered with existing activities and questions are posed about existing values.

Our final case differs from the first three in being concerned with a reduction in overall resources rather than an expansion. During the late 1960s and early 1970s a series of mistaken assumptions was made about the pattern which the birth rate was likely to follow. As a result, the number of live births was considerably over-estimated, and the number of teachers in training was discovered to be greatly in excess of requirements. So the colleges of education, having been subjected over more than a decade to constant pressure from the Department of Education and Science to expand, suddenly learned from the same source that they were required to contract at an even more rapid rate than they had grown. A relatively short time after the publication of the White Paper ironically entitled *Education: A Framework for Expansion,*[8] more than half the existing teacher training institutions had been scheduled for closure. Many of the remainder were required to merge with neighbouring polytechnics or further education establishments, or to federate with other colleges of education; a few were incorporated into university education departments; some of the larger ones were allowed to remain as free-standing colleges of higher education. The theory was that those which merged with technical colleges and polytechnics would offer a liberal arts element alongside the existing technological one; those which were established solely on a base of teacher education would diversify to offer other types of professional training as well as broadly-based arts degrees.

As in so many changes planned and executed by people who do not have to live with the consequences, the job proved in the event to be a badly botched-up one. Several hundred staff were made redundant or redeployed in occupations for which they had little enthusiasm. Several hundred others found themselves coping with the unsatisfactory consequences of a shotgun merger. In many cases the curricular blueprints sketchily outlined by the architects of the new deal never came to fruition. Even those staff who remained in teacher education continued to feel demoralized and insecure.[9]

It is interesting to speculate what would have happened if a sector of nationalized industry had been faced with threats of closure on the same draconian scale. One might guess that in the first place the government of the day would have been subjected to intense union pressure to subsidize uneconomic plants so as to keep them in operation; to embark on a major redeployment exercise which would guarantee new jobs in place of the old; and to gear the eventual rate of contraction to match retirements, voluntary redundancies, resignations and job transfers. Any serious attempt at adopting the tactics used for teacher education would certainly have precipitated a major political battle.

Within higher education itself, a politically more powerful sector of the system, such as the universities, would doubtless in comparable circumstances have been treated somewhat less peremptorily. Even if there were found to be a drastic shortage of students, or if resources had suddenly to be reduced while numbers remained constant, each institution would at least be allowed to work out for itself where the cuts should fall. In other words, those who made the ultimate decision would be those in the best position to calculate the full implications. It is perhaps a measure of how marginal the colleges were that there was so little debate about the possibility of allowing them to work out their own solutions, on the basis of attracting enough students on non-teacher courses to remain viable. Yet this could well have been a far less damaging, and not noticeably more costly, line of action.

Changes at the Institutional Level

Having seen how rarely it is possible to initiate successful changes at the level of the system as a whole, we shall now turn to consider the nature and effectiveness of innovations at the institutional level. We shall consider three main types of change in this category: those deriving from special interest groups outside the institution; those concerning attempts to modify the internal balance of power; and those relating to changes in academic or market demand.

Attempts at institutional reform on the part of special interest groups are now a familiar aspect of the higher education scene in Britain. One early example was the campaign to promote the use of closed-circuit television in undergraduate teaching, which enjoyed prestigious backing in the second half of the 1960s not only from a number of influential vice-chancellors but also from a special UGC committee on the use of audio-visual aids.[10] The educational television lobby succeeded in persuading a number of universities to invest in studio facilities as well as in specialist staff and equipment, but significantly failed to establish the medium as anything more than a marginal embellishment to traditional teaching provision. As a result, although there may be occasional lecture inserts and laboratory demonstrations on video-tape, and a modest use of televised reference material by students, few academics give any indication of considering television as a resource (on a par with textbooks and journal articles) to be closely woven into the fabric of the curriculum.[11] It would be rash to claim that the investment has anywhere near earned its cost, even a decade or more after its initial installation.

The same is true of most of the other developments in media and techniques which were clustered loosely under the heading of educational technology, and which ranged from relatively low-level technical innovations (the overhead projector as a superior substitute for the blackboard) to more far-reaching attempts to structure and evaluate course design through the introduction of behavioural objectives. The various pressure groups which promoted such innovations, and the brief waves of fashion which they enjoyed, were insignificant in comparison with the subsequent impact made by computer-assisted learning. The introduction of computers as teaching devices, particularly into the programmes of science and technology departments, seemed to make good sense. It was sponsored not only by commercial interests but also by a number of enthusiastic academics. Most of the facilities were already available and familiar; the effectiveness of the computer could be readily demonstrated, both as a tutorial substitute and as a means of simulating real-life experiments.[12] But even in this instance, despite a well-managed national programme during the early 1970s to promote experimentation and to encourage the widespread adoption of the findings, it is difficult to say that the outcome has been a major change in pedagogic practice.

By no means all the interest groups which have set out to sponsor institution-based reform have founded their approach on new media or techniques. To take one example, attempts to introduce or expand student counselling and advisory services have been promoted on a national basis by the relevant professional network. To take another case, there have been strong external pressures, from a variety of official and semi-official sources, for universities and polytechnics to introduce staff development programmes — the main argument being that academic staff often lack systematic training in teaching techniques and may therefore benefit from opportunities to improve their practical skill alongside their theoretical understanding.[13] In both instances — student counselling and staff development — the campaigns have come and gone, leaving behind an identifiable residue but somehow failing to transform the *status quo* in quite the way their proponents must have wished.

These examples of unsuccessful or only partially successful change, taken together, suggest that the efforts of interest groups outside the institution appear to go largely unrewarded. The same seems true, at least in part, of another type of change mentioned earlier — namely, innovation involving an attempted shift in the balance of power within the institution itself.

As a consequence of the student uprisings in 1968 and the succeeding years, nearly all academic institutions in the UK, as in other parts of the world, were under considerable pressure — both internal and external — to allow students a greater say in academic policy-making. In response to this, many universities and polytechnics created new departmental or course committees on which students were represented; they also allowed student membership of a number of existing committees. After a good deal of initial wrangling about 'reserved territory' (which protected certain committees or certain agenda items from student intrusion — for example, those dealing with staff appointments, assessment or discipline) the system appeared to settle down under the new dispensation.

It was not long, however, before disenchantment set in. Contrary to their expectations, student representatives appeared to wield little more power than before. In some cases, this was because the committees, especially those at the level of the basic unit, were not taken seriously by staff.[14] In others, it was because the process of academic decision-making turned out to be more complex and diffuse than the students expected: it was seldom a matter of a single determining vote at a clearly identifiable level in the organizational structure.[15] To make matters worse, there were increasing doubts about how representative of their constituents the students on committees were — a problem exacerbated by the apathy with which constitutional and policy issues were regarded after the mid-1970s, often resulting in a shortage of candidates and a disconcertingly small poll.

One outcome of these attempted changes in institutional power structure has been a shift of influence in a different and unexpected direction. Once students were given seats on important central committees, such as the senate and planning committee, the anomaly of excluding non-professorial members of academic staff became obvious and increasingly embarrassing. So more or less independently, in institution after institution, with relatively little in the way of protest or political pressure, minor constitutional changes were introduced to allow elected commoners into the academic parliament, alongside the professorial peers who sat there by right. The results of this peaceful and piecemeal erosion of the power of professorial heads of basic units have been far-reaching, for all that they have been so undramatic. The change has usually worked downwards to the level of the basic unit, where junior members of staff increasingly expect to have some say in policy issues affecting their own interest. In many cases, the headship of the basic unit is no longer a permanent appointment, but rotates between senior members at specified intervals (often five-yearly); in some, the appointee is elected and need not be of professorial or equivalent rank.

In this instance, at any rate, one may confidently claim that a lasting change has occurred — albeit one which was not consciously planned or lobbied for, but which emerged in the aftermath of another hard-fought but ultimately ineffective campaign. Our third and final type of change at the institutional level — namely that relating to academic or market demand — might similarly be judged as capable of a successful outcome. What is involved here is a generalized or specific pressure, acting on one or more institutions at any given time, whether from inside or outside, which ultimately gives rise to the creation of new basic units within the institutions concerned.

The internally generated pressures can be illustrated by taking the contrasting cases of biological sciences and computing. In the former instance strong academic arguments

were marshalled in the 1950s and early 1960s for amal-
gamating existing departments of botany and zoology to
reflect the newly-emergent concepts of a unified study of
living matter, embracing genetics, cell biology and ecology.
The organizational barriers in the way of achieving this
intellectual objective were, in many institutions, considerable.
Nevertheless, in a majority of cases the change happened,
and schools of biological science have become a more familiar
feature of the academic scene than the old pattern of separate
botany and zoology departments.

In contrast with this case of fusion of two existing basic
units, our next example illustrates what is perhaps the more
common process of the fission of one basic unit to produce
two. In the early years of the development of the computer,
the mathematics department seemed the natural base for
those teaching and researching into its applications. However,
as computing reached a state of academic maturity, in the
sense both of resting on a substantial body of specialist
knowledge and of generating intellectually important and
socially useful applications, the case for independence
became strong. Computer scientists had already established
their own peer network, separate from that of any of the
existing branches of mathematics; they had their own identifiable research interests; they had enough conceptual material
to justify teaching a distinct degree programme and enough
candidates to allow for viable recruitment. In short, they had
all the prerequisites for forming self-sufficient basic units
independent of their parent departments of mathematics.
Again, the necessary organizational changes were made, often
with some practical difficulty but seldom with any strong
intellectual opposition.

Alongside such examples of academic pressure, arising
predominantly within the institutions themselves, can be set
a different range of cases relating to external changes in
market demand. Where a new source of potential recruitment
and eventual employment appears, provided that the subject-
matter can be regarded as academically acceptable, there is a
strong temptation (particularly in institutions in search of
additional student numbers) to establish a new basic unit and
offer an appropriate degree programme. This tendency is
particularly marked in relation to vocational courses. Two

instances which come readily to mind are accounting and nursing studies, where the interest groups concerned have been generally successful in persuading institutions of higher education to offer graduate status to potential entrants to the profession. Although such innovations are liable to be viewed with greater suspicion than those arising from more straightforwardly academic sources, they can be readily enough accommodated in most institutions, provided that they establish their promise in terms of student recruitment and their acceptability in terms of intellectual substance.

In all the instances we have noted of change, or attempted change, at the institutional level, it seems reasonable to interpret success or failure in terms of our initial model. The first set of innovations (educational television, computer-assisted learning and staff development) not only derived from special interest groups outside the institutions, but placed their main emphasis on changes in the operational mode. They were able to win support at the institutional level to the extent of having resources earmarked to implement them: but the response from the basic units was usually less favourable. Even where the changes were adopted in operational terms, they did not succeed in establishing any change in the prevailing norms, and were soon discarded as 'no more than a gimmick'.

The second set of changes, namely, attempted modifications in the internal balance of power, related predominantly to the normative mode. Pressure, both internally and from external system-wide interest groups, persuaded institutions to modify their existing values, and consequently their modes of operation, to allow a greater role in policy-making first to students and then to non-professorial staff. But again, the majority of basic units were able to minimize the effect of student participation as being alien to their norms, even while accepting the enfranchisement of junior academics as compatible with their established values.

As to the third set of changes — namely, those involving the merger of existing basic units or the creation of new ones — we noted that the sequence of events differed according to whether the origins of the change were inherent in the academic enterprise or whether they represented reactions to external demand. Our examples in the first category were biological science as a case of fusion and computer science as a case of fission. In both these instances, a gradual but marked change in basic unit norms (reflecting operational changes in the pattern and direction of research) will lead eventually to changes in institutional values, and hence — through the reallocation of resources in the operational mode — create scope for the development of new curricula and staff configurations at the basic unit level.

In the second category, of response to market forces, we saw the pattern to be quite different, with the initial impetus coming from some external interest group. The first step has to be to ensure normative acceptance by the institution. If and only if this can be secured, the rest usually follows. The change in the institution's operational activities reflects the new set of norms (recognizing, for example, nursing studies both as academically acceptable and as viable in terms of student numbers), and gives rise to separate basic unit structures and budgets for curriculum development and research.

Changes Affecting the Basic Unit

Our analysis has already suggested that for the most part the basic unit occupies the centre of the academic stage. It is not surprising therefore to find that the pattern of actual and potential innovations at this level is richer and more varied than at any other in the system. Institutions may respond, more or less effectively, to suggested changes in their modes of support for teaching and learning or their decision-making structures; they may create new basic units and amalgamate existing ones. But there is not much they can achieve, as institutions, without the active support of their basic units. Central authorities, as we noted earlier, have even less scope for reform. Their main method of trying to install new values within higher education — or at least to ensure that changes in social demand are reasonably matched by changes in practice — lies in setting up new types of institution, closing down ones which appear to have served their purpose, or more often, through various inducements, investing institutions which already exist with new functions and purposes. In contrast, basic units, by virtue of being directly engaged with teaching (and in some cases also with research), have more immediate opportunities for innovative development, even if they do not always take them up.

We shall review six different patterns of change, without wanting to suggest that our catalogue is complete. They could be said, respectively, to exemplify changes in overall rationale; in curricular emphasis; in course structure; in disciplinary perspective; in teaching practice; and in assessment techniques. Each characteristically stems from a somewhat different source and reflects a different constellation of elements in the model.

The first type of change has already been touched on in earlier chapters. It usually arises from a major shift in values in the external environment of higher education — a shift which may not only call into question the established assumptions which lie behind a given basic unit's work, but also jeopardize its existence by reducing its attractiveness to students. There can, for example, be no denying the steady modification in intellectual climate over the past century which has demoted divinity schools and departments of theology from a major to a marginal role in university affairs. In consequence, many such units have chosen to reappraise their own internal norms, and to extend their function from the training of future members of the Anglican clergy to the provision of broadly-based comparative courses on world religions, with few if any vocational implications. This form of innovation is the more powerful for impinging simultaneously on the normative and the operational modes of the basic units affected by it: the more inexorable for giving rise not merely to changes in curricular provision but also to a search for a new ideology and *raison d'être*.

The second type of change, though less far-reaching, is occasioned in a similar way by modifications in the external environment. But in this case, the new element lies in the social or professional expectations invested in graduates, rather than in a broader or more pervasive value shift. Such a change more commonly affects vocational than non-vocational degree programmes, and is sometimes strongly reinforced by the outside body responsible for maintaining professional standards. A clear example is afforded by the inclusion in engineering curricula of a component which is meant to relate functional competence to an understanding of the social and economic context in which technological developments take place. The obligation to introduce 'engineering in

society' courses has been strongly pressed by the professional
engineering institutions, but it reflects a wider demand on the
part of employers that graduate engineers should have certain
qualities beyond narrowly vocational skills and a narrowly
technocratic outlook. The effect, in terms of our model, has
been for a new element in the norms of the wider peer group
to lead to a comparable reshaping of the norms of the basic
unit, and thence to shifts in curricular emphasis at the operational level.

Changes in course structure — our third category — can be
brought about in a number of ways for a variety of reasons.
The subset relevant to our present discussion is generated by
market pressures on recruitment. They characteristically
affect newly-established teaching programmes and also some
courses in institutions which have relatively low status within
the system. The problem confronting the basic unit involved
in such forms of provision is to compete effectively with rival
offerings which are of long standing, or situated within prestigious institutions. The solution involves seeking some
special means of attracting students, often by drastically
reshaping the conventional degree programme. Leaving aside
examples of this strategy at the level of the institution as a
whole (interdisciplinary courses in a number of the new
colleges of higher education; modular degree programmes at
many polytechnics, 'sandwich' courses interweaving academic
study with work experience at several technological universities), instances at the level of the basic unit would include
language programmes which abandon classical literature for
an emphasis on practical competence and an awareness of
contemporary social and economic developments; the introduction of 'degrees by independent study' in a handful of
polytechnics and new universities, and the adoption of a
'systemic' integrated approach to medical training, alongside an early introduction of clinical work, in some of the
recently established medical schools. The range of innovative
enterprises of this kind at the basic unit level is constrained
by institutional regulation as well as by the risk of disapproval
by the wider peer group. Nevertheless, the need for survival
in a competitive market can generate powerful internal
norms within the basic unit, leading eventually to institutional acquiescence and hence, in the operational mode,

to major innovations in the structure of the curriculum.

It may be useful to consider next a contrasting type of change, which — though often no less far-reaching — is generated entirely within the academic world and seldom has any external causal link (though there may in some cases be important indirect connections). We earlier referred to this fourth species of change as one in disciplinary perspective. What we have in view is not the straightforward accretion of new ideas and materials which constitutes the everyday task of research, technology and scholarship, and which duly finds its way into the currency of the undergraduate curriculum. It is, rather, that more remarkable process referred to by T. S. Kuhn and his followers[16] as a change of paradigm: a substitution, in our terms, of a substantially new element for a significant part of the existing norms of a whole academic peer group. Changes in this category are in fact closely comparable with the internally generated realignment, at the institutional level, of basic units such as biological sciences and computing, to which we referred in the previous section.

Changes which involve the reappraisal of an academic subject area as a whole are rare: those involving a particular sub specialism within a broad field are relatively more commonplace. One recent example of a major shift in paradigm, or set of disciplinary norms, can be found in geography, where the old territorial disposition of physical geography on the one side and human geography on the other has been largely superseded by the imperial claims of a new discipline based on quantitative techniques of spatial analysis. This has given rise to significant changes in the nature and content of courses — changes reminiscent of earlier, though more limited, influences on mathematical teaching from the development of set theory; on physics from the establishment of relativity theory and the uncertainty principle; and on social history from the importation of the techniques of demographic analysis. Such changes might be claimed to constitute the essence of the academic enterprise, even though they involve a limited range of components of the system as a whole. The process characteristically starts in the operational mode with new patterns of research, whose findings in their turn affect peer-group norms in the wider scholarly community. Once the new norms are sufficiently established at the level of the basic unit, they begin to be translated back into the operational mode in terms of changes in the nature and content of courses.

The last two sets of changes we shall consider at the level of the basic unit are also predominantly internal, though less far-reaching in their impact on the curriculum. Both tend to arise from a sense of disequilibrium between the normative and the operational modes (see the earlier discussion in the first section of this chapter, 'The process of innovation'); but one is typically inspired by academic staff, while the other will more usually be generated by students. The staff-initiated changes are those which give rise to new forms of teaching practice: here we have specifically in view the pedagogic innovations which affect the operations of the basic unit, in whole or in part, rather than those which are restricted to the individual level. Examples would include the adoption of project work as a significant component of the undergraduate curriculum; the exploitation of small-group techniques in place of lectures; the development of independent learning schemes; or the introduction of substantial elements of 'concentrated study' in which one particular topic is pursued exclusively — that is, with no other competing courses — for a sizeable block of time.

Very often, the origins of such developments can be put down to serendipity, and their justification to improvements in the quality of life. That is to say, the staff of one basic unit may pick up an apparently interesting idea through contact with the staff of another unit — or have it imported through the arrival of a new faculty member at a fairly senior level — and may eventually agree to put it into effect.[17] The (relatively minor) adjustment in group values will often be achieved by the argument that the change in question will result in a significant improvement in current practice, and thus enhance student motivation as well as increasing the job satisfaction of the teachers concerned. From that point, it remains to put the new norms into operational effect (a step which, while it may in some cases call for a fairly major investment of staff effort, is usually undertaken with some enthusiasm once the conviction is there).

The main characteristic of student-initiated changes, understandably enough, reflects the basic currency of undergraduate life. As we saw in Chapter 7, the individual norms of students are strongly conditioned by the system by which they are assessed for degree classification. So for them, a major source of improvement in job satisfaction must lie in a reduction in the anxiety caused by examinations and other forms of assessment. The number of changes in assessment procedure over recent years suggests that the academic world has recognized the legitimacy of student views in this domain. The majority of innovations — such as the increasing emphasis given to course work assessment, the introduction of 'take-away' and 'open book' examination papers, and the availability in some programmes of alternative methods of assessment between which individual students can choose — have originated in some form of student initiative, whether based on confrontation or negotiation.[18] Here, of course, the mechanism is somewhat different from that for staff-initiated changes, since it focuses predominantly on change in the operational mode (whereas the crucial element in staff-initiated change is in the normative mode) and is brought about by the organization of dissent (as opposed to the creation of consent).

Although we would not claim that these six distinctive processes of innovation account for all possible changes at the level of the basic unit, they may at least serve as a reminder of the wide variety of ways in which new academic developments can occur. As we have seen, basic units can be subject to internal as well as external pressure. Such pressures will in some cases generate a major change in both normative and operational modes; in others the effect will be discernible largely or exclusively in the operational mode (representing an accommodation to an external threat rather than a fundamental shift in values).

We have put forward no examples of changes which impinge only on the normative mode and leave the operational mode unaffected. This should not be surprising in the light of the earlier discussion, in the first section of this chapter, of the general nature of innovation. If the collective values of a particular basic unit change, the need to give tangible expression to those values constitutes a powerful incentive for a commensurate change in the practice of that unit. The only effective hindrance is likely to come either from the external peer group (which is liable in the end to have its way, if it cannot be converted or divided) or from the institution (which will usually be worn down, or may manage to drive some compromise, but which will seldom achieve outright supremacy). However, the argument need not be laboured here, since it is only another way of making the point which has already recurred a number of times about the relative strength and importance of the basic unit within the system as a whole.

Innovation and the Individual

There is in one respect a good deal to be said about the role of the individual staff member or student in promoting or responding to change — and in another respect comparatively little. Clearly, even though a basic unit, or an institution, or the whole higher education system, is somewhat more than the sum of its parts, it is none the less largely dependent on the co-operation of those parts. And if one is to avoid the trap of reifying organizational entities, it has to be remembered that individuals, in one role or another, go to make up not only the various basic units in an institution but also the institution itself, and (so far as academics are concerned) a substantial part of the network of central authorities as well. There is a sense in which all reference to innovation in higher education *ipso facto* involves reference to academic teachers and those they teach. Nevertheless, there is a clear distinction between talking about a given student *qua* representative on the departmental course committee or *qua* member of the senate, and talking about that student specifically as an undergraduate following such-and-such a course. Equally, it is important in any analytic study of higher education to differentiate between a given staff member *qua* head of department or member of planning committee, or chairman of the mathematics subcommittee of the UGC, and that same staff member when functioning as a teacher on such-and-such courses or as a researcher in such-and-such a project team.

In the present discussion, we shall concentrate on the second alternative; namely, that in which teachers and taught are viewed in their role as particular persons. This is not because we want to belittle the importance of the other functions which they may fulfil, but because most of what can usefully be said about them is already implicit in our earlier account of changes at the levels of the system, institution and basic unit. The exploration of the model will, however, remain incomplete unless we extend the analysis to the fourth and most fundamental level, namely, that of individuals within the system.

We immediately come up against a number of factors which limit the scope of what the individual can do, how far he or she can depart from established practice, and how far he or she can bring about collective change. The external constraints are perhaps obvious enough not to need much discussion. The most powerful, as suggested in our model, are the collegial group norms which map out, for the members of any given basic unit, the acceptable range of professional beliefs and the expected style of conduct for those at different levels of seniority (undergraduate; postgraduate; junior staff; senior staff). There are also — though they are generally taken to be less significant — quasi-contractual constraints which impose certain minimum levels of commitment at the operational level, such as hours of teaching for staff and hours of attendance at lectures, seminars and tutorials for students. The details can be elaborated to include problems of the allocation of personal time and effort as well as the broader issues of disciplinary allegiance and identity.

But despite these curbs on individual action, even the most junior academic and the most recently recruited student retain a fair degree of liberty — the first to determine how he will present the required curriculum content within a predetermined structure, and the second to decide how he will set about acquiring the understandings needed to satisfy his eventual examiners. In so far as the choices call for departures from established practice, the personal and educational values of both teachers and taught are likely to be crucial components in the effectiveness of the consequent change.

Individual attitudes and wants are sometimes hard to separate out from externally imposed disciplinary ideologies and professional loyalties, and perhaps even harder to distinguish from allegiances to particular educational viewpoints. None the less, each academic and each student, in his capacity as a human being, has certain notions of right and wrong, good or bad. He also has some personal preferences as between one kind of activity and another, and his own particular idea of what it means to be doing a worthwhile and rewarding job. These various considerations will colour his judgement of any new and unfamiliar proposal. Thus, for instance, an academic strongly committed to research and relatively uninterested in teaching is likely to show little enthusiasm for developing a programme of 'skill sessions' in undergraduate physics practicals which promise to be time-consuming to work out. Similarly, a teacher who believes strongly in preserving the authority of staff members will be reluctant to embark on the democratic procedures inherent in some forms of seminar activity. (Overall, one might say, because of the well-defended expectations of academic freedom in most institutions of higher education, the individual academic's power of veto is a more potent barrier against change than his power of assent is a force in support of it.)

The analysis of curricular traditions in Chapter 6 has already underlined some key distinctions between educational value systems, including the differing implications, at the basic unit level, of a positivist stance and a relativist position. A somewhat comparable contrast can be marked at the level of the individual between those who, explicitly or implicitly, see teaching issues in terms of developing an appropriate technology — which implies the existence of discrete entities, absolute values and clear-cut causal conditions for change — and those who, consciously or unconsciously, emphasize the organic nature of the educational process — which carries with it the notion that learning is complex, contextually sensitive and essentially unquantifiable. The former view gives little weight to the educational milieu; the latter regards it as extremely important, and holds that phenomena which are abstracted from it will lose many of their crucial characteristics.

Clearly, differences in basic educational value of this kind generate quite different responses to various types of curricular innovation. For example, those who take a holistic perspective are unlikely to look kindly on courses with a tightly programmed structure based on closely defined behavioural objectives, or to favour a modular curriculum pattern. In contrast, those who take an aggregative view of knowledge will tend to have little sympathy with the psycho-dynamic overtones of small-group learning, or with the integrative aspirations of interdisciplinary degrees.

Given the complexity of the relationships between each academic's personal, educational and professional values on the one hand, and the demands made by different forms of pedagogic and curricular innovation on the other, it may seem surprising that change ever happens. Two considerations help to explain why it does. First, it is inherent in the notion of academic community that mutual accommodations and working compromises should be sought even where they are not accompanied by any significant shift in value position. (Were this not so, it would make adequate teaching provision virtually impossible: any curriculum must have at least some sense of convergence, and in the majority of cases it has to be achieved by negotiation between individuals with different priorities.) The second consideration stems from the relative success which most people have in matching themselves to their environment. When a new member of staff is appointed (or a new student enrolled) to a basic unit, it is usually as a result of a skilful, though unacknowledged, process of mutual choice. So it is much less common than it would be by random selection to find a maverick individual whose values are strongly at odds with those of his immediate academic colleagues. The resulting tendency towards a consonance of group norms, at least at the level of the basic unit, is something to which we shall return in our subsequent analysis of the scope and limits of change.

Strategies for, and Barriers to, Innovation
Having begun with a theoretical account of the process of change in terms of our model, and then continued with a more detailed analysis of the limits and potentialities of innovation at each level of the system, we end by bringing the various strands together so as to present some kind of synoptic pattern, however sketchy and incomplete.

Before we embark on this exercise, it is necessary to re-mark that we see no reason whatever why academics, any more than other people, should embrace novelty merely for the sake of novelty. If a particular course is attracting a large surplus of good, well-qualified applicants, and the teachers responsible for that course are well satisfied with it, then they should not be expected to tinker with it merely at the behest of a self-instruction enthusiast or a devotee of inter-disciplinary inquiry, any more than most of us would change our jobs merely on the advocacy of an employment bureau, or sell up our homes solely on the urging of an estate agent. We noted earlier in this chapter (see pages 135–6) that institutions and basic units sometimes introduce major curricular reforms in response to the need to attract students to newly established programmes or courses which are relatively low on the pecking order of recruitment. The other side of the same coin is that the higher up the ladder of disciplinary pres-tige a particular group of teachers may be, and the more reputable their institution, the less likely they are to want to institute any far-reaching innovations in curricula or teaching methods. If well-established basic units often appear staid and conservative, that could be because a natural corollary of satisfaction with one's own status is satisfaction with the *status quo*.

Nevertheless, the historical perspective of Chapter 3 should serve as a reminder that times change rather faster than in-stitutions, and that, outside the world of higher education, political fashions and economic climates come and go with little regard for the well-being of academia. The problems with which the system, and its constituent institutions and basic units, are now expected to contend are almost un-recognizably different from those which faced the much smaller and in some respects more insulated network of universities a generation ago. The degree of autonomy which they assumed, and the strong sense of freehold which indi-vidual academics felt able to enjoy, have few parallels in contemporary higher education. Instead — largely no doubt (and rightly, perhaps) as a result of the almost exclusive dependence of universities, polytechnics and colleges on public funds — the present-day system is called upon to defend its legitimacies and demonstrate its responsiveness to market pressures in a way which would have seemed unimaginable in the immediate postwar years. But whether or not externally derived innovation is thought to be a good thing, it is arguable that it has always been an endemic feature of the relationship between higher education and its wider environment.

It may be helpful for the purposes of analysis to distinguish between four broad types of change stemming from outside the system. (All of them should be seen as quite distinct from internally inspired pedagogic and curricular changes, such as those discussed in pages 136–8 above.) The first two impinge mainly on the operational mode; we shall label them respectively as 'inexorable' and as 'prescriptive'. The third and fourth mainly affect the normative mode; we shall refer to them as 'radical' and as 'evolutionary'.

By inexorable change we mean that type of adjustment which institutions, or basic units, or even individuals find themselves being forced to make in their pattern of everyday activity as a result of external forces which are largely or entirely beyond their control. One example at the institutional level would be the way in which the pattern of first-year teaching would have to be reshaped if there were a major change in school sixth-form curricula and examinations;[19] an example at the level of the system as a whole would be the changing recruitment pattern, age distribution of students and course structure resulting from the demographic decline in the early 1990s. We have already mentioned numerous examples of inexorable change (chemistry, classics, and so on) at the level of the basic unit. Such innovations tend to be viewed in somewhat the same way as minor natural disasters — that is to say, they are accepted in a fatalistic spirit rather than actively resented. They may have only a negligible, or at most an indirect and gradual, effect on individual or collective norms: but even where the old values remain intact they will be played out in a very different way in the operational mode. There is no contesting the effectiveness of this kind of change: it is change for survival.

In contrast, what we have called prescriptive change meets with neither success nor acceptance. It constitutes that type of innovation — usually involving some major organizational overhaul — which is projected for some reason or another by a more general on to a more specific level in the system. A good example is to be found in the Swedish U68 reforms, which arose from the attempt to superimpose community values on academic values, and resulted in a root and branch reshaping of the structure of higher education in Sweden. The subsequent legislation has unified the administration of universities and colleges at the central level; interposed, for some functions, regional bodies which are predominantly controlled by industry, trade unions and local politics; and devolved much academic decision-making on to elected groups within the institution. Almost invariably, such managerial attempts to modify the current operational patterns of institutions, or basic units, or individuals (or all three at once) alter the established distribution of power in unforeseen ways, and give rise to a series of unpredicted side-effects. They tend to be strongly resented and to make no substantial impact on existing values (except in so far as they cause a deterioration in morale). Even at the operational level, those affected by them are liable, according to circumstance, to reject them outright, to resort to camouflaged evasion, or simply to go through the necessary motions in a mechanical way. Thus, returning to our Swedish example, the number, frequency and variety of systematic changes are claimed by some critics to have resulted in a 'decision death' at the lower level of the basic unit and a resort to the 'quiet life game' at the level of the individual academic.

Our next category, of radical change, probably needs little explanation. It is normative in its emphasis — that is, it focuses primarily on values and only secondarily on forms of organization or patterns of activity. We reviewed a number of innovations of this kind earlier in the chapter (especially on pages 129–32). One example at the level of the system was the attempt to infuse the polytechnic sector with a distinctive ideology; another at the level of the institution was the endeavour by students to establish their right to participate in policy decisions. In the majority of such cases, innovative ideas are likely to founder because they go too far in challenging established assumptions. Those who prefer to hold to the existing norms, and who thereby emerge as opponents of change, are not necessarily to be dismissed as obscurantist. They may quite reasonably estimate the costs of abandoning known values as greater than the benefits of espousing unknown ones.

Finally, we come to evolutionary change. This again makes its main impact in the normative mode: but its distinctive characteristic is that is succeeds in maintaining a strong continuity of values in one direction while introducing a significant discontinuity in another. Thus, as we noted on page 125, the Open University won acceptance at least in part through its clear determination to match the standards of excellence of more conventional UK universities. Given that it could not be faulted on the stringency of its assessment criteria, academic opinion not only allowed it to get away with the flouting of other established conventions, but in certain cases followed its initiative. Similarly, at the level of the basic unit, the recognition for assessment of undergraduate project work — despite its apparently radical departure from existing practice — rapidly became an established element in the curriculum, because of its conformity with another familiar and respectable practice, namely, the examination of graduate theses. Innovations which manage in this way to challenge certain accepted ideas while reinforcing others have a fair chance of success, provided that they also meet two other prerequisites: that their merits are reasonably visible and that they do not appear seriously to undermine the existing patterns of freedom and control.[20]

Taken together, our four categories of externally generated change suggest a somewhat negative stance on the part of academia and the academics towards innovative ideas. The numerous examples we have cited of internally initiated change at the level of curricula and teaching approaches should help to offset the static and unresponsive image which higher education might otherwise seem to project. Nevertheless, it remains the case that many changes, including those generated from within, fail because they are unable to accommodate to existing structural constraints. Academic structures and regulations for the most part evolve to protect the legitimate interests of researchers and teachers. They help to define, and also defend, the main areas of professional concern within an institution. But once established, they can prove surprisingly intractable. Even when an innovative idea is generally accepted on intellectual grounds, it may face severe difficulty if it appears to conflict with conventional practice, or to cut across some existing

organizational arrangement. Its eventual success will depend
not only on collective agreement among those likely to be
directly involved in its implementation, but also on collective
persuasion of those whose role it is, at the institutional level,
to monitor and approve the resulting activity. The latter may
see the enterprise as threatening to their own interests or as
demanding of resources which they are not themselves prepared to yield up. And those whose normative task it is to
ensure the maintenance of proper standards may veto the
proposals as providing insufficient evidence of academic
rigour.

On this analysis, the conservatism of British higher education is somewhat exaggerated by its critics. We have argued
it to stem mainly from contextual rather than from personal
factors. It cannot, as is often claimed, be ascribed to the fact
that academics are inherently reluctant to depart from the
ways in which they themselves reached intellectual maturity
(as a psychological generalization, this is implausibly naive).
The main constraints on change are social, not psychological:
they depend more on the way the system operates than on
the particular stand that its individual members choose to
take.

9. Evaluation, Accountability and the Allocation of Resources

Evaluating and Accounting

Chapter 6 was concerned largely with an analysis of the vertical links in our model: namely, those which connect a normative element at any given level with its operational counterpart. In this chapter, we shall be looking at the contrasting set of horizontal links in the model: namely, those in the normative mode which we have labelled as being concerned with judgement, and those in the operational mode which we have designated as having an allocative purpose.

We shall need first to distinguish, in relation to the judgemental functions exercised by one level over another, between the two connected but different notions of evaluation and accountability. We will attempt to show how each of these notions can embody a variety of different value stances, some tending to be more readily acceptable at one level in the system, and others at another. Finally, after examining the impact of demands for evaluation and accountability on the elements of the model in the normative mode, we shall go on to look at the related allocation procedures deployed in the operational mode.

Although evaluation and accountability are closely interrelated, the relationship is not symmetrical. That is to say, accountability presupposes evaluation but evaluation does not necessarily imply accountability. It would be not merely odd but positively unacceptable to hold individuals or institutions to account for what they have done or failed to do without first trying to make an informed judgement of the merits of their performance. But it is quite common to make judgements of performance which are not then used to call individuals, or basic units, or institutions, or the system as a whole, to account.

The nature of the distinction is somewhat akin to that between balancing one's books and having them audited. The former is a matter of working out debits and credits; the latter involves not only an independent scrutiny of the results but also the prospect of punitive or ameliorative measures if some irregularity is found. An accountability procedure may or may not lead to a formal inquiry into the causes of those effects which are deemed unsatisfactory: but it must by definition make some provision for retributive (or, at best, remedial) action.

The notion of accountability thus entails some procedure for institutional action in relation to those who are judged to have fallen below acceptable standards. It may be seen as a means of translating the results of an evaluation process into practical effect — perhaps by refusing approval or recognition, perhaps by withholding resources or changing the conditions of their availability, or possibly by making public the relevant details about inadequate performance.[1]

With these distinctions in view, we shall start by examining the different functions which evaluation serves at the different levels of higher education, and then go on to tackle the more politically charged issues of accountability.

Styles of Evaluation

If one looks at educational evaluation as a whole, it is possible to discern three quite common, clearly distinguishable, types or styles. Each generates its own particular techniques and procedures, and each embodies a different world-view. In characterizing the three in turn, we shall label them as instrumental, interactive and individualistic.[2]

The instrumental style is recognizable as the one most popular — at least until relatively recently — among those classifying themselves as professional evaluators. It aspires to the impartiality, objectivity and universality of classical physics, holding that by the careful introduction of measures for comparison and control, educational situations can be treated as on all fours with those in a laboratory investigation. Instrumental evaluations are hospitable to the concept of clearly defined and measurable objectives, whether in relation to curricula or to broader analyses of policies. Their reports usually adopt the passive mode fashionable in scientific writing, and are liberally interspersed with statistical correlations, reports on tests of significance and numerical measures of phenomena which might otherwise have been thought to defy quantification.

It is important to clarify the basic value stance which underpins this particular approach. In emphasizing the comparability of educational phenomena with those of physical science, it counts people as objects, whose behaviour is in principle explicable in terms of a series of natural laws. Instrument evaluation also rests on the implicit assumption that nothing can be truly said unless one can put a number to it.[3]

Turning next to the interactive style, this might best be characterized as based on the anthropological paradigm, in much the same way as it was suggested that the instrumental style took its prototype from classical physics. Evaluators in this genre seek to underline rather than to play down the untidiness and the particularities of the educational context which is the subject of their scrutiny, and to involve themselves in it rather than to distance themselves from it. They seek out the atypical as well as the typical instance: their aim is to portray the differences in perspective between those who take up different roles in the situation. They tend to be chary of numerical measures and hostile to the notion of breaking up broad policies into specific objectives. Their writings are generally informal in style, though occasionally interspersed with the terminology of the social sciences. Such writings often embody analytic distinctions derived from the writers' own data, which have some implicit claim to applicability in other situations.[4]

The underlying value stance in the case of interactive evaluation embodies a view of people as social animals, conforming to no absolutes and obeying no universal rules, and yet capable of being understood within their own terms. It maintains that judgements cannot be derived from objectively determined criteria or rigorously applied measures: where they have to be made, they must be seen to depend on the adoption of a particular frame of reference.

What we earlier labelled as individualistic evaluation has a very different set of characteristics. Its methodology is perhaps nearest to that of narrative history. The individualist evaluator is at the other end of the spectrum, in terms of the generalizability of his findings, from his instrumental counterpart. His insistence is on the uniqueness of the particular instance: everything is what it is, and not another thing. As he sees it, the evaluator's task is to document a careful case-study, in which the significant reality of the subject under review is faithfully portrayed. In so far as any conclusions may be drawn, they are those relating to *general* human situations (that is, ones which are recognizable in many people's experience) rather than to *generalizable* claims about humankind (that is, ones which purport to be universal). A case-study, like a novel, a play or a fable, may serve to point a moral: but it must never be taken as proving a rule. Those who espouse this particular type of evaluation typically cast their written accounts in a descriptive and documentary form, untainted with technical terminology of any kind.[5]

The individualistic evaluator might be described as adopting a romantic value position. It is rarely, if ever, that he can be coaxed into taking any judgemental stance, maintaining that the quest for empathetic understanding should render judgement unnecessary. If, however, some brash administrator or politician should insist on attaching a price tag to what is necessarily a unique educational enterprise, it must be his own responsibility to reach a judgement, on the basis of the evidence which the evaluation provides. All judgement is irremediably subjective: there can be no pretence of attaining the objectivity which instrumental evaluation proclaims, or even of achieving the intersubjectivity to which interactive evaluation aspires.

In delineating these prototypes, we have chosen to compare and contrast them through the activities of that relatively small group of people having some kind of professional concern with educational evaluation. This approach has the advantage of sharpening the outlines of each portrayal: but it is misleading in its implication that the evaluation with which we are here primarily concerned is professional in nature. In practice, the large majority of evaluative activities in higher education are carried out not by educational evaluators but by those whose interests, skills and responsibilities lie primarily elsewhere. In so far as people are called upon to reach judgements of merit and worth, they do so in virtue of the particular role they occupy within higher education, rather than because of some special competence they are thought to possess in the techniques of evaluation as such. Nevertheless, we shall attempt to show in our subsequent discussion that the three basic styles of approach outlined above — intrumental, interactive and individualistic — reappear in different contexts as part of the day-to-day workings of the system, and are not confined merely to the marginal activities of those who consciously style themselves as evaluators.

Formal or Professional Evaluation

Various reasons can be put forward to explain why higher education rarely uses outside experts in appraising the quality of what goes on. An obvious one is a generalized distrust of evaluative methods, coupled with a disbelief in the validity or relevance of the findings to which they give rise. Another, at the level of the basic unit, is the long-established view that teaching is an essentially private activity, from which it follows that it is unseemly to expose it to the view of others. Yet another, at the institutional level, is a reluctance to set aside any significant resources for evaluation, on the basis that even if it is not an impossible business, it is certainly not necessary nor worthwhile.

However, there are occasional cases in which someone independent of a particular activity and not in membership of the relevant peer group is invited or commissioned to undertake a review of it, rather as a management consultant might be called in to reappraise the functioning of a commercial company. Such examples need to be taken into account, even though they are relatively few in number.

In nearly all instances, external, professional evaluations focus on innovative developments, because new initiatives are much more often called upon to justify themselves than are existing practices. There is no intrinsic reason why a long-established procedure should not be reviewed critically from time to time (though there are various extrinsic reasons why it is not — for example, that the teachers concerned are in a strongly entrenched political position, or that neither they nor their colleagues nor their students have any serious doubts about what they are doing). But as things are, those academics concerned to resist change or — more reasonably — to ensure that it is not change for the worse, are sometimes in a position to press strongly for novel departures to be introduced on sufferance and with the proviso that their functioning should be reviewed after a given interval. In contrast, programmes which have been in action for several years may never have been systematically appraised, even by those directly responsible for them. To say this is to make the same point in a different way — that formal evaluation is only a marginal aspect, not an inherent feature, of British higher education.

The least-neglected domain is that related to teaching and learning activities at the levels of the individual and the basic unit. There has been a long and sterile tradition of comparative studies, often carried out by educational psychologists, of the relative merits of lectures versus programmed learning, seminars versus television teaching, and the like. Investigations of this kind are often generated or commissioned by agencies outside the basic units involved. They are almost invariably inconclusive (showing 'no significant difference' between one approach and another); they tend to ignore both the context and the content of learning; and they are for the most part based on a pointlessly scientistic research design. It is scarcely surprising that they have made little difference to practice or prejudice.

The evaluation of complete courses is somewhat less common, though from time to time a basic unit may commission an independent review of a course offering, particularly where it is a new one under trial, or where there are already plans to redevelop an established programme in some far-reaching way. Externally commissioned studies of whole institutions are rare.[6] The majority of institutional evaluations have been confined to particular inquiries about deep-seated problems, and have tended to take the form of internally-sponsored committees of inquiry rather than of more technical evaluation exercises. (Examples have included a review of the constitution of the University of Birmingham,[7] an examination of internal academic structure at Cambridge[8] and an inquiry into the overall functioning of the University of Oxford.[9])

There are also occasional attempts made to conduct some form of evaluation at the level of the system as a whole. These are usually limited in scope to one particular type of activity (such as, for example, computer-assisted learning),[10] or confined to a somewhat naive input-output design (as in some economists' attempts to compare the cost-effectiveness of one set of institutions — say, the polytechnics — with another — say, the universities). However, in the individualistic, case-study tradition, there are also what might be called evaluative accounts of central institutions such as the University Grants Committee.[11]

But taken all in all, the amount of formal evaluative activity throughout the system is limited. It comprises a miscellany of instrumental, interactive and individualistic approaches, yielding nothing which comes anywhere near to giving a coherent and systematic analysis of what works and what does not, what is up to standard and what falls below it. Information of this latter kind remains to be generated by less self-conscious exercises in evaluation, albeit ones which are embedded firmly in the routine procedures of the enterprise as a whole.

Judgement and the Individual

Higher education is as poor in impersonal evaluation as it is rich in personal judgement. To substantiate this claim, we shall start by discussing the nature of judgements which take place at the individual level, and then go on to examine the judgemental connections between each pair of successive levels.

One of the most familiar forms of personal judgement is that made by a tutor of those students whose progress he is responsible for overseeing. As part of the task of guiding and supporting them in their exploration of unfamiliar intellectual territory, he may from time to time remark on the quality of their work, with the intention of helping them by his comments to improve. The same individual may, however, have a different, and in some respects conflicting, function at the end of the programme. As one of their examiners, he may be required to help ascertain and certify the quality of his students' academic accomplishments at the point at which they present themselves for final assessment. From being an adviser and a critical but friendly commentator he has to become an impartial judge; in so far as he starts as a coach, he ends as an umpire. (This is an unusual conjunction of responsibilities in most areas of human enterprise, but it can in fact be seen as a recurrent pattern in higher education.)

A tutor's interim judgements of his students' work, where these form no part of the formal assessment procedure, are not normally subject to supervision or direction by the basic unit. They are taken to be as much matters for his personal discretion as are his day-to-day decisions on how to present the course he is teaching. It is interesting therefore to observe that there are three fairly clearly distinguishable strategies, which correspond to the distinctions drawn on pages 149–51 above between instrumental, interactive and individual styles of evaluation.

Those tutors who adopt an instrumental approach tend to think in terms of absolute values, and hence to calibrate students' efforts on a scale which is seen as independent of context and completely impartial. Just as they strive for a universal and external standard of excellence against which to measure final examination scripts, so they see it as their task to identify and use that self-same standard in relation to the possibly halting efforts of a first-year student.

It is rather more common for academics to adopt the interactive stance characteristic of relativistic values. Coursework assessment is allowed to be dependent on the general context, different degrees of expectation being seen as appropriate for different stages in the course. In so far as students are measured against a criterion, it tends to be that of the average performance of their own group rather than some quite extrinsic consideration.

There is, however, a third strategy adopted by some tutors (and usually frowned on by the rest). It consists in applying individualist values to the process of marking coursework, and judging each student in terms of his own normal level of performance. If a weak student does well in relation to his past efforts, it may be psychologically important for his piece of work to be rewarded with a high grade. Equally, if a normally very able student does badly by his previous standards, the fact should be signalled by a low grade. So one student might get an A for a piece of work which, if handed in by another student, would only rate a C.

The difference between the first two positions and the third marks a major ideological division between those teachers who emphasize the need to preserve some sort of constancy of judgement in marking coursework and those who see this as comparatively unimportant. The latter consider work which is not formally assessed as promoting the interests of the students as learners, and see their own task as building up the students' confidence by giving individually tailored appraisals that might help to improve subsequent performance. The former see coursework marks as serving the longer-term needs of the students by giving them periodic indications of their performance levels and showing realistically how far they rise above or fall below the standards required (be these relative or absolute).

Formal student assessment for degree awards does not allow for such *laissez-faire* divergencies, since it is subject to a whole range of institutional constraints. We can perhaps most conveniently review it in the context of the judgements made at the basic unit level. Before going on to consider the relationships between individuals and basic units, however, it remains to be noted that the higher education system allows very limited scope for judgements of individual staff members by students. Some inferences about what such judgements would amount to can be drawn from the student comments on the quality of courses which are encouraged by some basic units. However, the type of staff popularity rating exercise which was introduced in a number of US universities and colleges in the aftermath of the 1968 student troubles never caught on in the UK. Quite apart from the vigorous staff opposition which such a procedure aroused when it was first officially proposed,[12] the students themselves have, perhaps understandably, a greater reticence in appraising the quality of teachers than the teachers show in appraising them. In extreme cases, a student may make a formal complaint about a member of staff, or perhaps less directly request a change of course or of tutor. But such implied judgements are entirely in the individualistic style, and do not have reference to any more generalized interactive or instrumental values.

Appraisal as a Way of Life

In considering the judgements made between basic units and
individuals, we shall begin by looking at the student population. Basic units have a prime responsibility for the final
assessment and certification of their students, and an obligation to their wider peer group, their institution and society
at large to ensure that the judgements reached are fair and
equitable. There is, as we have already remarked, no question
of permitting the kind of individualistic values which are
able to survive at the level of the tutor's personal appraisal of
coursework. What, then, is the characteristic value stance
behind degree assessment?

Any answer to this question must distinguish between
rhetoric and reality. In the case of many basic units, the
official answer would indicate an uncompromisingly instrumental position. It would be asserted that clear standards
existed, independent of the unit itself or of any other contextual factors, and derived purely from considerations of
specifiable competence in the subject-matter. The inherent
implausibility of this assertion does not prevent it from
being earnestly and sincerely advanced. It undoubtedly
portrays a state of affairs which would be wished for by
quite a few academics. However, two considerations serve
to undermine it, the first theoretical and the second practical.

First, every academic programme is highly complex and
capable of being followed with a great degree of variation.
Leaving aside the majority of courses which permit the
student to opt for particular emphases or particular themes,
there is no single course whose assessment at degree level
comprises a set of examination papers with no choice among
the questions posed to candidates. So, strictly speaking,
no one group of students ever has an exactly identical performance requirement for all its members. The variations
between different groups — be they contemporaries in different institutions or successive cohorts in the same basic unit —
are naturally even greater. If a degree in archaeology, say, had
the same simple structure as a boy scout badge for camping
(with a number of clearly specifiable tasks to complete at a
defined standard), it would be reasonable to say it was assessed
in an instrumental style by absolute criteria. As it is, the only
conceivable way to deal with the kind of complexity involved

is to resort largely to relativistic, interactive procedures, and to rank students impressionistically in relation to their peers.

Second, it has often been demonstrated in practice that the distribution of degree classes shows a pattern whose consistency can only be explained by assuming the operation of what are called, in the ungainly jargon of educational research, norm-referencing procedures (that is, those in which a particular and specifiable distribution of results is expected, or engineered, around an average level defined in relation to the group concerned). Any given basic unit shows a remarkably constant pattern in its classifications from year to year; the characteristic patterns for (say) mathematics degrees throughout the system are quite easily distinguishable, and are markedly different, from those for (say) philosophy; and even the aggregated classifications for institutions as a whole remain surprisingly stable over time, and differ predictably between one institution and another.[13]

There are powerful reasons for overlooking such arguments, in terms of a desire to maintain parity of value for all degrees. Nevertheless, it would seem reasonable to conclude that the basis for degree assessment, while clearly not individualistic, is not instrumental either — and that it does in fact reflect the approach which we earlier described as interactive.

In recent years, a new dimension has been added to the relationship between the basic units and their students. While students have always been judged, they have only in the past decade or so been given the opportunity to sit in judgement in their turn. That is to say, a significant number of basic units now invite, or even solicit, student comments on individual courses and on the curriculum as a whole.

The origins of systematic appraisal of courses by undergraduates, as of many other academic reforms, lay in the radical movement of the late 1960s. At that time, a number of student unions organized 'underground prospectuses' each offering some form of consumers' guide to the courses available in their own institution. These were predictably condemned by the proper authorities as dangerous and irresponsible: but on careful scrutiny, some at least were found to be reasonable, balanced and helpful in advising new applicants.[14] The idea eventually gained ground that students — who were among other things expected (and sometimes explicitly trained) to develop sound judgement — were in fact capable of exercising that competence in commenting on their own academic fare.

The case for such critical appraisals of curricula can be supported on grounds of general principle. Even where all the teachers on a given degree programme try carefully to co-ordinate what they are doing (which is by no means a universal practice) they are not able either individually or collectively to know at first hand what the course as a whole comprises. They cannot know this, because each only sees directly that part of the course which he teaches. The actuality of what colleagues do has to be inferred indirectly from discussions about syllabus, comments from students, and the like. In contrast, the students, individually and collectively, do experience all or nearly all the separate components as a complete entity. It is only they — or the rare members of staff who take the role of students and sit in on colleagues' teaching — who are actually in a position to aggregate the components and to say whether they fit together in a sensible and coherent way. On this argument, then, students more than anyone else have the opportunity of assessing whether the degree programme is the meaningful entity which its planners and providers intend it to be.

In any event, judgements of this kind by individual students of the basic unit's curricular provision are collected in a variety of ways — for example, by routine questionnaire on the completion of each course, by detailed interviews of a sample of students each year, or by requests for reflective essays from recent graduates. In most cases the purpose is to inform the basic unit of possible or necessary improvements. The proportion of cases in which the resulting information is acted upon is less easy to determine. Students' judgements, in terms of our threefold categorization, are clearly individualistic. They are not normally in a position to compare the courses they have taken with provision on other degree programmes in their own, let alone in another, subject area. Few of them would have the confidence to claim access to a set of external and objective standards in terms of which teaching programmes could be definitively assessed. At best, they can aspire to a personal response to a unique experience.

Individuals and Collectives

Quite another kind of judgement is involved in the normative interactions between basic units and their constituent members of staff. The relationship will of course vary, depending on whether the purpose is formal or informal. In the UK there are comparatively few occasions in the career of an average academic when formal evaluations have to be made about teaching or research competence (the position is quite different in the USA). Although some universities review all staff at regular intervals to assess their potential for promotion, for the most part such appraisals are confined to initial selection for membership of the unit; the granting of tenured status to new entrants to the profession; the decision to award some form of approved status (as in cases where an 'efficiency bar' operates for salary increases); and specific proposals for promotion from one level in the hierarchy to another. In such cases there are formal procedures, largely dependent on the operation of appropriately constituted committees (consisting of academic peers both inside and outside the unit in question).

In contrast, there are numerous occasions when some informal – perhaps not even explicit – evaluation of individual strengths and weaknesses has to be made. Many such evaluations will be related to the allocation of tasks in either the teaching or the research domain; others will involve selection for some activity outside the basic unit (such as an institution-wide committee or some conference involving the wider professional network); others again may lead to decisions about the granting of special facilities (leaves of absence, secondment, extra resources for research, and the like). The procedures for reaching judgements of this informal kind are seldom constitutionally defined. Their nature will depend largely on how any given basic unit is organized: the relationship of the unit with the individual may lie anywhere on the range between a collegial appraisal (approximating to the process of wider peer-group assessment) and a hierarchical and authoritarian judgement by the head of the unit.

The inverse of the process – the judgement by individual academics of the basic units to which they belong – has no clear status other than, if strongly negative, to encourage the disaffected individuals to find a more congenial occupation. The most obvious route of escape is to a comparable or more senior post elsewhere: but this route becomes constricted, if not virtually closed, in times of retrenchment. Other possibilities have then to be sought, which may include a switch of effort into institutionally based (and predominantly administrative) tasks or into some form of academic political activity.

Moving beyond the basic unit to the wider scholarly community (which is to say into the external environment which contains our model, but is not portrayed in it), we have already remarked in Chapter 6 on the important influence of 'invisible colleges' and special interest groups in certain academic domains. The distinctions made earlier between research, technology and scholarship are particularly worth recalling here. It is certainly the case, for example, that a chemist who is awarded a Fellowship of the Royal Society on the basis of judgement by eminent fellow chemists on the excellence of his work is thereby certified in the eyes of academia at large to have scaled the higher reaches of his profession. If any doubts existed about his competence on the part of colleagues in his basic unit, this judgement would be deemed to override them, and even to cast doubt on the academic competence of such colleagues. But the same does not hold for membership of those outside bodies whose function is to monitor standards of technological or professional competence. Their special concern is with the training of new entrants, and hence indirectly with the efficiency of basic units. They do not offer awards to practising academics which enjoy much outside currency and prestige: their more prestigious forms of recognition (for example, fellowships of the Royal Colleges in medicine) are largely reserved for leading practitioners, rather than for those who provide an initial academic training in their field.

When it comes to academic units giving their main emphasis to scholarship, particularly in traditional arts subjects, the operation of the peer-group network is even less clearly defined. The British Academy is not able to exercise the same degree of influence on the central authorities as the Royal Society does; nor are its activities awarded equal credibility by the academic world at large. Scholarly standing on a national or international basis has for the most part to be acquired without the help of a public and formal reward system: as we argued earlier, it tends to be heavily dependent on the processes of publication and critical review.

Questions of merit and worth necessarily have a more fine-grained texture when they relate to individuals, or to relatively small groups of colleagues, than they do when they concern larger and more impersonal entities. Evaluation at the level of the central authorities and the institutions is of necessity broad and generalized, and thus not amenable to as close a form of analysis as is called for in reviewing the mutual appraisals of individuals and basic units.

In the nature of the case, institutions are not as knowledgeable about the specialisms which they collectively provide as are the basic units which individually provide them. So each academic judgement which an institution has to make in relation to its basic units is made from a position of comparative ignorance. It is for this very reason that the confident subjective (or more accurately, intersubjective) judgements made at the levels of basic units and individuals have to be replaced, on an institutional scale, by self-consciously objective and procedural assessments. Where, as in a given academic field, there is a shared language, and often a large corpus of shared cultural understandings, it becomes relatively easy to do without elaborate cross-checking, or formal appeal mechanisms. But once one moves into a domain in which there is no convergence of values — once, in fact, there is a degree of pluralism which makes it impossible to use procedures which rest on reaching a consensus — the more elaborate quasi-legal machinery of arbitration, negotiation and conciliation has eventually to be wheeled in. In terms of our threefold classification of value stances on pages 149–51 above, the institutional approach is predominantly instrumental, moving whenever possible from qualities to quantities, from seeing people as people to regarding people as things.

As was remarked in Chapter 4, the central authorities do not suffer to the same extent from these institutional burdens of ignorance and the consequent need for procedural objectivity. They are in the first place able to draw extensively on the expertise of wider peer groups in framing their judgements about the relative merits and demerits of different basic units.

In the second place, if they do happen to make mistakes, they do not have to live with them at such close quarters. And in the third place, because they are the ultimate dispensers of resources within the system, there is a prudential disincentive to quarrel with them too loudly or too long. All this is not to suggest that decisions at the central level are irresponsibly made, or frequently erroneous: it is merely to underscore a number of obvious but important differences between institutions and central authorities. The contrast is marked by a resulting preference, centrally, for the interactive mode of evaluation, in which placing institutions and basic units in a rough order of relative merit is a more familiar exercise than attempting to match them accurately against some notional standards of academic excellence.

Some General Implications
It is evident, from our review of the range of evaluation procedures at different levels in the system, that although individualistic and instrumental approaches have some scope (especially the former at the individual level, and the latter at the institutional), the main pattern is the interactive one. This tendency to prefer — or at least to go for — relative rankings of one element against the rest, rather than for some absolute standard or a merely personal and ungeneralizable appraisal, is perhaps only to be expected, given the nature of the academic enterprise. Higher education is, as we have already suggested, too complex to permit the drawing-up of any simple objective criteria; equally, the notion of generalizability is inherent in almost every aspect of its function.

One unusual feature of evaluation procedures in higher education has been remarked in our discussion on student assessment on pages 154–5 above: namely, that those called upon to act as arbiters will normally have quite other roles (which seem in certain cases to be inconsistent with, or at odds with, the evaluative function). Many internal examiners are simply the course teachers and tutors in a new and temporary guise; equally, those who sit on today's tenure and promotions committees are yesterday's and tomorrow's friends and colleagues. Even at the level of the institution and the central authorities, as the discussion in Chapters 4 and 5 makes plain, individual academics are co-opted to help reach decisions which may affect colleagues in their own basic units, whether for better or for worse. The requirement for some academics (and especially the more senior, experienced and established ones) to adopt a series of different roles at different levels in the system is perhaps an inevitable consequence of the high value placed on specialized academic knowledge in this system, as opposed to many other areas of public policy. It means that a straightforwardly hierarchical system of management, with evaluative decisions flowing down from the centre through the institutional elements to the individual, is ruled out of court. Given the tenet that only experts can properly assess cases made by fellow experts, it follows that the jury of peers is the most appropriate mechanism to adopt.

Successful as this collegial mechanism has in general proved to be in academic evaluation and governance, it is of necessity less detached than are the more bureaucratic or autocratic devices employed in other contexts. The evaluation has an impact, not only on those who are evaluated, but also on the evaluators: for the latter are, at the end of the day, at one with those they evaluate. At least, they are within the same extended family (or even perhaps within the same nuclear family): and when a family's circumstances change — whether by the discovery of a black sheep in their midst or by the identification of a white hope — all the members of that family are affected to some degree, if only by public association. So those who are unable strongly to compartmentalize their views, and to distance themselves from their everyday loyalties and affiliations, are left with a curious form of dual existence, in which they have not only to demonstrate the impartiality of their evaluation, but also to keep in view its consequences for themselves and their intellectual kin.

Despite these difficulties, it has to be acknowledged that the traditional evaluation mechanisms have a positive effect on higher education, and meet the needs of the system far better than alternative processes would be likely to do. They have the advantage of helping to keep open to view many of the activities of individuals and basic units, and of strengthening them through the process of collegial scrutiny. They also contribute the essential evidence for questions of accountability, to the examination of which we shall now turn.

Accountability in Academia

The demand for accountability in higher education often stems from the view that academic instituions ought somehow to certify that they give good value for money. This latter notion may be interpreted in two (related but different) ways: first, as a requirement to demonstrate economic efficiency; and second, as a need to show that high standards are being maintained in relation to the calls of the system on public expenditure. We shall look at the implications of each in turn.

'Value for money' is normally established in terms of some fairly straightforward criterion which can be used to demonstrate whether a given enterprise is achieving what it is supposed to achieve. From our account of higher education in Britain, it should be obvious that no such criterion exists, or could be invented. If the network of academic institutions were more unitary, and more closely bound up with a single ideology, it might be possible to identify a consistent set of policy goals and to examine the extent to which they were being attained. As it is, there is no real sense of shared purpose and no simple method of measuring the achievement of such purposes as can be discerned.

The only sensible lines along which any general appraisal can proceed must be in terms of what the system is actually like. We have already argued that its corporate values are weighted in terms of the autonomy of specialist groups within each institution. We might usefully look at the system in terms of the contrast between mediaeval craftsmen and the large conglomerate enterprises which grew up as a result of the industrial revolution. Higher education in Britain has not experienced any counterpart to industrialization: it remains a loose network of small enterprises built around a marketable specialism.[15]

It is easy enough to rehearse the nature and terms of reference of a public debate on whether Britain's motor industry has sufficient potential to justify ever-increasing government subsidies. The arguments involve complex value issues (such as the implications of massive unemployment for car workers) as well as differing views of what the relevant economic projections should be. But the *components* of the discussion are relatively few, and relatively manageable. Imagine now an attempt to reconstruct a similar debate about carriage-making in seventeenth-century Britain (when each large country town had its own modest firm of carriage-makers) or even about the thousands of ox-cart-builders in contemporary India. The fact that each craft co-operative would have its own distinctive style of approach, that it would manage its own budget and deal directly with its own clientele, would make it highly problematic to assess the rights and wrongs of possible public subsidy. Some co-operatives would have high standards and others dubious ones; some would be efficient and others incompetent: it would be far more difficult to generalize than it is between Leyland, Ford and Chrysler. If one were to increase the complexity by attempting to account for all the different forms of local manufacturing (boot-makers, potters, blacksmiths, and so forth) taken as a whole, the effects would be reasonably comparable with those of a requirement to undertake an efficiency audit of the total system of universities, polytechnics and colleges.

One obvious way of introducing better accountability would be to impose a much greater degree of centralization: not only, perhaps, a single management system, but also a common set of target requirements (and hence by implication a central admissions policy and a nationally specified curriculum). After all, there are already more countries which adopt some such practice than those which do not. As with our earlier example of the motor industry, if the number of separately accountable elements could be minimized, and some reasonably coherent and measurable goals could be spelled out, the problem of evaluating the system as a whole would at least become manageable.

However, centralization brings losses as well as gains. The length and the strength of the British tradition of academic independence would minimize the gains and emphasize the losses. One of the main objections, among many, is that central control would make the system less capable of adapting to changes in circumstance. At best, it would substitute one kind of rigidity — that of the central authorities — for another — that of the basic units. And given the notable failure of manpower planning techniques in the UK during the 1960s (when they were in high fashion and enjoyed powerful support), it seems unlikely that decisions about target outputs made by government could offer any improvement at all on the present situation. Those who argue for preserving the existing *laissez-faire* structure would point to its capacity for a reasonably rapid and sensitive response to the type of degree programmes which qualified applicants want, even if this may at some times be at the expense of leaving industry short of a particular type of required expertise, and may at other times be at the risk of leaving highly trained people to find jobs unrelated to their academic courses.

It therefore seems more appropriate to seek accountability in terms, not of the large corporation, but of the co-operative of craftsmen. Instead of attempting to identify overriding goals and evaluate how far they are being achieved, or to specify clear-cut criteria for the efficiency of the enterprise as a whole, it makes better sense to ask how standards are set and maintained, and how far in general the customer's needs are satisfied.

In relation to the latter criterion, the merely quantitative consideration of how far higher education succeeds in maintaining a healthily expanding undergraduate population by being alert to market changes and responsive to new growth points has to be offset by qualitative considerations. It would be possible so to devalue academic qualifications that virtually anyone could acquire a degree: but that, as the traditionalists point out, is not what higher education is about. A degree, if it is to have any credibility at all, must represent a certain publicly recognizable standard of performance. In Britain that standard is established and safeguarded by a network of protective measures (external examiners for university degrees and the careful machinery of the Council for National Academic Awards — which also includes external examiners — for degrees in the public sector). Such measures are intended to ensure that every degree course, regardless of the institution in which it is taught, ends by requiring of its students a level of achievement broadly comparable, within the limits of human error, with every other degree course in every other institution.

In the case of an institution which is not chartered (as universities are) to award its own degrees, any proposal for a new course, or for a substantial change to an existing one, has to survive a series of hurdles. The first is internal to the institution, and involves convincing relevant colleagues about the academic viability of the scheme. The second calls for a review in terms of resource planning rather than educational desirability, through the machinery of approval of the Regional Advisory Council within whose domain the institution falls. The RAC's prime interest is in questions of cost, available staffing resources, degree of overlap with existing provision in the region, and estimated student numbers. The third and final testing point is referred to as validation, and takes one of two forms. The longer-established but currently much less common alternative is to seek external degree status at an affiliated university, usually in the same geographical region. The more usual option is to apply for the course to be recognized for the award of degrees by the Council for National Academic Awards.[16]

The CNAA validation procedure is basically quite simple. Every proposal is scrutinized by a panel set up for the purpose. The scrutiny is designed to be rigorous and severe. The procedure as a whole, being based on the widely recognized principle of peer-group review, is by and large accepted throughout the higher education system. Panel members — there will usually be up to a dozen — are drawn from university and polytechnic staff in the relevant subject fields; there will also be one or two academics from neighbouring disciplinary areas and one or two well-informed outsiders from industry or elsewhere. Each panel member will have very full documentation about the aims of the course, the teaching approaches and forms of assessment proposed, the qualifications of the academic staff, library and laboratory resources, and teaching accommodation. The CNAA panel makes at least one 'site visit' lasting a whole day (or more) to cross-examine the team concerned with the proposal and to look at the relevant facilities. Where it is not satisfied on a particular point, it may designate a sub-panel to make a further visit, or call the proposers to a meeting in the Council's headquarters. Eventually, it will recommend acceptance of the proposal, decline it, or refer it back for amendment and resubmission.

Once a course is approved, the CNAA, though aware that there is likely to be a certain gulf between the original plan and its eventual execution, does not exert a close control over minor deviations. It does, however, require to be consulted over more substantial modifications. It also appoints the external examiners for the course as well as approving the internal examiners, so retaining a check on standards of student performance. Since it is the Council that actually awards the resulting degrees, it is in a good position to insist that the course be brought back into line if it appears to have deviated significantly from it. The Council also requires as a matter of routine procedure that every recognized course should be reappraised at five-yearly intervals. This is done in the same way as initial appraisal, involving updated course documentation and a full site visit by an appropriate panel.

In contrast, degree proposals which arise within the universities themselves have a relatively easy route to recognition. All the negotiations are internal: the first necessity is to persuade departmental or divisional colleagues that the scheme is worth backing; the second, to meet the requirement of other groups in the same faculty that the innovation will not make unreasonable calls on resources that would otherwise come their way; and the third, to satisfy the senate that the proposal is academically respectable and in accordance with proper standards. Once these negotiations are completed, it remains only to appoint new staff (as need requires and finance allows), to nominate external examiners and to recruit students. No outside agency has any voice in this procedure, except in courses leading to professional qualifications. No review after five years or any other period is demanded. The documentation required to launch a new proposal is typically brief — dealing mainly with syllabus and assessment procedures and saying little about teaching methods and resources. The exercise has the casual informality of a family housekeeping budget rather than the procedural rigour of a company audit.

Despite their procedural differences, the universities and public sector institutions nevertheless share an insistence that their degree awards should be at essentially the same level. This preoccupation with rigorous standards is a mixed blessing. It does a good deal to preserve political credibility in a system which, because it lacks clear goals and any obvious criterion of efficiency, is otherwise vulnerable to criticism. In the face of attack, the colleges, polytechnics and universities can at least point out that many more under-graduates now reach honours standard in their courses than was the case ten years ago, and hence that while the quality of output of higher education remains constant, its quantity has increased disproportionately to the increase in real cost. But the awkward truth which this *apologia* does its best to conceal is that there are, in reality, no absolute standards of achievement. There is no way of ensuring that an upper second-class award in philosophy at Bristol is set at much the same standard of difficulty in 1979 as it was in 1954, let alone of confirming that any third-class degree in history in one university is comparable with any third-class degree in mathematics at another university.

Leaving aside the fact that an insistence on absolute stan-dards conceals a need to rely on relativities, the inflexibility of the degree currency makes it difficult for unorthodox and unestablished subjects to gain a foothold (in marked contrast with the US system, which allows degrees from different institutions to establish their own value in the market). It also, by limiting acceptable coinage at the undergraduate level to a single denomination, reduces the attractiveness of higher education to students who would prefer a shorter than normal time-span, or who for other legitimate reasons wish to leave their courses at an earlier stage, or who might in cer-tain subjects reach their 'academic ceiling' after, say, six terms. In other words, the demand for the maintenance of standards tends to give rise to a tendency towards standardi-zation, which in its turn inhibits the capability of the system to respond in an imaginative way to changing circumstance.

This pushes the argument back towards the North American system, in which the gold standard of academic awards is abandoned in favour of a floating currency. In the USA, first degrees are publicly acknowledged to denote very different levels of academic achievement, depending on whether they are conferred by an institution high up a fairly commonly agreed pecking order or one nearer the lower end of the scale. Although the standards set by any given university may be expected to remain more or less constant over time, there are opportunities in the free play of a competitive market for each and every institution to gain or lose prestige, to win a better reputation, or to lose an established one.

There are reasons — particularly in terms of limited resources and a demographically changing student population — to expect that the British system will be constrained to shift in this direction. In so far as it does, its accountability will have to be assessed in terms of its responsiveness to student demand rather than its maintenance of predetermined standards.

It is noticeable that no specific mention has been made of individuals, basic units and institutions; nor has the question been raised how they might be deemed accountable in a way analogous with the system as a whole. There is good reason for this omission, in that little needs to be said. Once the argument is pitched at the levels at which professional activity has to be judged and justified — namely, those relating to individual staff members and basic units — the direction of accountability is unmistakable. The only possible means of auditing a high degree of expertise is through the independent application of the same expertise. That is why the mechanism of the peer group is so pervasive a feature of the academic way of life. It is also why specialists, whether singly or in their institutionalized groups, will acknowledge the firmly established right of other members of their guild to hold them professionally to account, but will deny that right to anyone else. Such accountability as individuals yield to basic units, or basic units to institutions, has to be defined in narrowly procedural terms.

If basic units and individuals are thus privately but not publicly accountable, institutions are in a somewhat different case. In so far as their predominantly academic norms — the maintenance of due process and the initiation of developments — are in question, the same professional considerations apply as for their component units. But when it comes to their general fiduciary role, and their responsiveness to central demands, they are open to external testing as part and parcel of the total system. A symbolic acknowledgement of this public liability was made in 1967, when the then secretary of state (Anthony Crosland) decreed that the accounts of the universities, which had hitherto been monitored by their own lay governing bodies and their own auditors, should be opened to the inspection of the government's Comptroller and Auditor General.[17] Although this new departure was greeted with a certain amount of horror at the time, it has since become an accepted element in the accountability of academia.

The Allocation of Resources

Both evaluation and accountability have important consequences in terms of the allocation of resources: which is to say that the horizontal links between the elements of our model in the normative mode cannot be seen as entirely independent from the horizontal links in the operational mode. Nevertheless, there is seldom a perfect harmony between the two — and the extent to which they fail to reflect one another could be taken as one measure of the degree of inefficiency of the system.

Any evaluation is in some sense an appraisal of how well needs are being met. If it is favourable, it suggests that the available resources of manpower, materials and money are adequate to the task in hand; if it is not, there will usually be some implication that more facilities are needed, or that the existing ones should be redeployed.

Accountability is quite explicitly connected with retribution and reward. If an individual, or a basic unit, or an institution, is found to have fallen below the required standard, then the person or persons concerned, according to circumstance, must either be prepared to be penalized by some reduction in the resources already available to them, or hope to be compensated by some increase in those resources. If, similarly, an individual, basic unit or institution is found to have risen above the required standard, then the expectation will be that excellence will be rewarded by some special privileges.

In practice, rewards and punishments are more often meted out in terms of changes in public reputation (which have themselves an important effect on such basic resources as student numbers, research funding and the like) than in terms of any direct changes in recurrent budgets or staffing norms. As we noted in Chapter 8, those whose task it is to allocate resources — whether at the level of the central authorities, or the institution, or the basic unit — have relatively little room to manoeuvre, except in a time of major and rapid expansion, since most of the budget at any level is already predetermined by commitments from which it is difficult to disengage.

The major scope for changes in resource allocation is at the level of the central authorities, whose task it is to deploy the overall budgets of the system in terms of their own evaluations of institutional merit and need. Even in a time of economic stasis, they are able if they so wish to impose small-scale cuts, either across the board or differentially, in order to support those developments which they consider to be necessary or highly desirable. But the agencies who exercise control at the national level do not exist in a political vacuum. The institutions at the receiving end of their decisions are capable of protesting vigorously at what they take to be unfair or mistaken policies. In any case, as we noted in Chapter 4, many such central agencies themselves have academic members, partly in order to ensure that what they propose is not too far out of line with prevailing academic values. So the freedom of central authorities to determine changes in budgetary emphasis, though important for the long-term development of the system, should not be overrated in the short term.

Academic institutions, in a system of devolved responsibility such as that of the UK, have a major role to play in deciding how the overall funds allocated to them should be divided between their constituent units. It is possible to distinguish three broadly different approaches to institutional budgeting. We shall denote them, respectively, as oligarchic, bureaucratic and collegial. They echo, but do not accurately mirror, the instrumental, interactive and individualistic styles of evaluation discussed at the beginning of this chapter.

Oligarchic budgeting procedures take two possible forms. In an institution with a powerful head (of which a few still survive, although the species is rapidly nearing extinction) it can sometimes be the case that the annual budget is straightforwardly allocated on the basis determined by him. This is clearly the simplest way of proceeding: but unless the leader's authority is never open to question, it tends to give place to the second form of oligarchic allocation, based on a contest between robber barons. The latter approach allows the beneficiaries of the budget to carve it up between them, usually by appointing to the institutional finance committee all the heads of basic units. But this procedure, though ostensibly fair and reasonable, does in fact discriminate in favour of those units fortunate enough to have a head who is a good entrepreneur and can drive a hard bargain, and against those whose head is naive or inept in financial debate. It also provides little scope for entirely fresh initiatives, such as the establishment of a new basic unit, since each unit's spokesman sees it as his primary task to maximize his own allocation rather than to create new sources of demand on the budgetary total. The 'every man for himself' principle is not one which — especially at a time of limited or zero growth — creates either a just distribution of resources or a climate receptive to new development.

Some institutions, in an endeavour to eliminate the internal dissention to which oligarchic budgeting arrangements can give rise, have introduced bureaucratic processes designed to make resource allocation as automatic as possible. Under such systems there is no academic discussion of priorities or rights and wrongs: the central administration simply redistributes any budgetary increase or decrease on a formula basis to individual units. There are two assumptions (both usually mistaken) behind this bureaucratic style of financial management: first, that the historical baselines are adequate; and second, that no significant changes take place in the relative requirements of different units. The policy of hiding budgetary problems under a cloak of arithmetic impartiality may succeed in buying temporary peace, but the final conflict is likely to be all the greater (as in one actual instance, where a department of physics and a newer and expanding department of electrical engineering in the same institution had similar laboratory requirements and virtually identical student numbers, but where it was discovered that the former's budget was no less than three times larger than the latter's).

Collegial procedures in budgeting (as in other activities) involve making all the relevant information publicly available, and establishing a common basis of agreement by negotiation. One such procedure calls for the production of a chart or matrix, showing the total full-time equivalent students for each basic unit (allowing for the part-time teaching of students from other departments as well as the teaching of any part-time students attached to the unit in question) plotted against each degree course. Budgetary funds are earned at an agreed per capita rate for undergraduates (the rate being higher in laboratory than in library subjects); research students are also costed at a higher figure. The budget allocations in the basic matrix are open for general debate. They can form the starting point for a series of further discussions. In some variants of this approach there is a small tribunal of reasonably independent academics which receives proposals from interest groups for new academic initiatives and requests by basic units for budgetary increments for which some special case can be made. The tribunal modifies the original matrix figures in the light of its adjudication of these claims, and publishes its recommendations. An appeals procedure can be invoked by any claimant who feels that his case has been unjustly treated; the final figures are then ratified by the appropriate committees.

There are two particularly important features of this third approach. It brings budgetary discussion from behind its conventional mask of secrecy and takes it out of the exclusive control of the power elite; it also creates the necessary institutional space for promoting new academic developments. It is much less easy for bureaucratic formulae or oligarchic free-for-alls to do this. Such procedures bear hardest on those activities which are newly established, vulnerable, innovative and closest in touch with contemporary student needs. By making it difficult — if not impossible — to implement in practice even those new developments which are established as worthwhile, they help to ensure that the pattern of course provision remains set in a changeless and increasingly outdated mould.

Turning next to the level of the individual academic, there are certain fairly specific forms of provision which have an important bearing on the teacher's and researcher's job satisfaction, and the absence of which can seriously inhibit him in his work.[18] Obvious examples are secretarial services and library holdings. But these are familiar enough issues to anyone responsible for running a basic unit, and tend to be given proper attention. What is sometimes forgotten is the opportunity that exists, in most institutions, to take advantage of peculiarities or irregularities in the accounting system: for example, computer facilities are sometimes a central charge and are therefore a 'free good' as far as basic units are concerned, whereas other facilities are directly costed. Another issue which tends, mistakenly, to be overlooked, is the potentially high value for low cost of such fringe benefits as unit-based funds for entertaining visitors and for travel and conference fees. The staff mobility which is promoted in this way can, when sensibly managed, help to create greater national and international visibility for the basic unit as well as a wider reputation for its members.

While questions of resource allocation give rise to a variety of issues, one of them is perhaps more important than the rest, since it lies at the heart of the problem of how the system adapts itself to changing external needs. As we have noted, the particular dangers at a time of retrenchment are that units peripheral to the main power structure continue to be afforded only peripheral resources and therefore lack the opportunity for healthy and natural growth. A case-study (which, though fictional, is derived from a real instance) may serve to illustrate the point and underpin the moral.

A large provincial university decided, in the early 1970s, that it would institute a new department and provide undergraduate teaching in a relatively novel branch of the social sciences. The impetus came in part from the expectation of lively student demand for courses, and in part from the enthusiasm of some members of the existing social science faculty, who saw the area as an intellectually challenging one which they themselves wished to develop. There was full agreement in the senate that a chair should be established in the subject and that the necessary complement of staff should be built up to form a new department. An appointment to the chair was in due course offered to an up-and-coming academic from another university, who prudently sought — and was given — firm assurances from the vice-chancellor that the initial rate of growth of staff and associated facilities in the new department would be rapid enough to ensure a viable scale of operation, and that subsequent expansion would keep reasonable parity with the growth of student numbers.

The appointment was accepted on that understanding, and

the new professor moved in alongside the three existing staff members who had opted to transfer to the embryo department. Perhaps all would have continued satisfactorily had not the first of a series of increasingly severe cutbacks been imposed on the higher education system at the very moment when the department's first additional post was to be advertised. The institution (in common with many others) took the defensive step of 'freezing' all new posts, and this delayed the acceptance of the department's first undergraduates by a year. When the new post was actually offered, a year later, it became clear that this was now being regarded by the university as the limit of the department's expansion for the time being. Its staffing complement was barely adequate to service the planned undergraduate intake; the recruitment of any doctoral students or the development of any programme at master's level was out of the question. The head of department, understandably enough, considered there to have been a breach of faith. The vice-chancellor was obviously embarrassed to have gone back on his word, but powerless to do anything about it. To make matters worse, the other facilities being offered to the department in terms of accommodation and recurrent funds were manifestly inadequate. The professor, as head of a very small unit, had no direct access to the planning and finance committee machinery, and his protests in the senate were largely ignored by other departmental heads, who had their own budgetary troubles. Four years after the department was established, it had its maximum agreed intake of students, but a lower level of resources than would be necessary to ensure healthy survival. The staff were under considerable strain, and the departmental head felt frustrated and disillusioned.

There is, of course, an element of sheer bad luck in this catalogue of events. The university in question had been in a phase of steady expansion for something approaching twenty years: it was used to initiating fresh ventures and paying for them out of the regular increments in its budget. It had no experience of, and no particular incentive to institute, procedures for funding new developments out of cuts in expenditure on outdated activities. It did not see the necessity, when the decision to start the new department was first taken, to set aside funds earmarked for its future growth — as before, such growth was to be paid for out of future budgetary increases. Nor did the university in question, when the crunch came, have the sort of financial machinery which would make it possible even to levy a small reduction in the funds of all other departments in order to protect and subsidize the new department.

This particular example of short-sighted management is far from atypical of higher education. It underlines the weakness of the peer-group principle as applied to the allocation of institutional resources — and incidentally to institutional evaluation and accountability as well. Academics, though conscientious in framing judgements within their own areas of expertise, show little commitment to making sound decisions about the issues which affect the running of their institutions. It is as if the practitioner is so closely allied to his own practice that he cannot give sensible attention to political and organizational problems in the wider context; as if loyalty to the basic unit imposes a balkanized and fragmented view of the enterprise as a whole.

10. Adapting the Model to other Social Policy Areas

The Main Themes Summarized
The model presented in this book illustrates how the components of the higher education system, and the system as a whole, work. The general propositions implied in our model must be tested and amplified, as the preceding chapters have shown, by the use of historical data, by taking apart the components that are necessarily stated in global form in the model and by placing them within their social and political environment. The model also stands to be tested in terms of its ability to help describe and explain the dynamics of change and the mechanisms of evaluation, accountability and the allocation of resources and tasks.

We believe that the central components of our framework are applicable to other institutional settings. The purpose of this chapter is to adumbrate its wider potential. In so doing, we will first remind the reader of the main themes of our argument before applying them, in sketch form, to analogous examples of processes and structures in medicine as practised in hospitals, social work as practised in fieldwork, and school teaching as practised in secondary schools.

We began by distinguishing between values, as expressed in the normative mode, and activities, which comprise the operational mode. The usefulness of applying this distinction is both conceptual and managerial. Its application to the case of higher education in the earlier chapters has exemplified the commonplace that there are conflicts and differences in values according to the standpoints of different participants. We have also illustrated how the normative and operational modes relate to each other. The aim has thus been to identify both the why (values) and the how (operations) of one particular public service, and to state the linkages between the two.

Our concern is partly intellectual and partly practical. In the last decade there have been several examples of the large-scale reorganization of public institutions in which functions have been carefully specified in the operational mode but in which the values underlying work at different levels have been taken for granted, and hence ignored. This was true of the reorganization of local government and of the national health service in the early 1970s. In consequence, we would argue, there has proved to be a demoralizing dislocation between what people hold in esteem and what the system requires them to do.

From the differentiation between norms and operations our analysis moved on to consider what constitutes a viable level within a larger system. Although we have typified levels in terms of such institutional artefacts as 'basic units', the analysis is primarily concerned with the functions that might be incorporated within levels. For a level to be viable, be it an individual, a basic unit, an institution or central authority, it must have identifiable values, expressed through a distinguishable normative mode, characteristic functions, expressed in the operational mode, and a discernible quantum of authority and discretion.

Having established the two main axes of our model, we showed how norms and operations are linked vertically and how the various levels are linked horizontally. In Chapter 8 we suggested that a predisposition for change is created when the normative and operational modes at any level in the system become significantly out of phase. The horizontal links in the model, as delineated in Chapter 9, are, in the normative mode, those concerned with judgement which become effective through the processes of evaluation and accountability; and those in the operational mode concerned with the allocation of resources.

These components of the model provide a notation through which to describe and analyse certain key policy issues. Throughout virtually every public service area, the relationships between central authorities, institutions and units are constantly under test, and accommodations are made between different levels of such systems, through different patterns of relationship.[1]

Applications to other Areas of Social Policy

With these components of our model in mind, we now turn to consider how they might be applied to other fields.

We have already noted the three areas in which we propose further to develop our model: teaching within the maintained secondary school system, hospital medicine within the national health service and social work within social services departments. These examples have been chosen because they are all activities within public welfare systems; because they all involve different types of interaction between individual practitioners and their clients; because they all embody problems about the relationships between different institutional levels; and because they differ widely in the ways in which authority to carry out tasks is distributed. But although we are here confining attention to three instances, we would expect the model to be capable of adaptation to any complex institutional system.

Problems concerning the stratification of systems[2] arise in each of our three sample areas. In this section we apply our criteria to the determination of the numbers of levels and then ask about the relationships between them. We have supported our claim that there are four levels in higher education by analysing discernible sets of values, with associated tasks for each. But there is not necessarily the same number of levels in all systems: the actual structure has similarly to be determined by the number of definable value clusters and their associated functional distinctions.

Hospital Medicine

A hospital doctor within his firm or department (perhaps the nearest equivalent to the basic unit in higher education) may work in a hospital within a district, which has its own management team. The district management team refers to an area health authority, which employs all members of staff other than senior doctors, who are employed by a regional health authority to which the area refers. The region refers to a government department. On the face of it, all of the professionals within that structure, and not only doctors, work within a structure that contains at least six different levels. But when we apply the criteria contained in our model, of values, functions and authority, we find that there are only three, or at most four, distinct levels, despite there being many more organizational *tiers*. The tiers exist to co-ordinate those services that cannot be administered economically in smaller groupings. It is acknowledged that hospital consultants must work according to their own norms, the better to serve the individual patient: but since hospital medicine is extremely expensive in human, physical and financial resources, it is also required that different specialties must work cohesively in the treatment of the individual. So the basic unit within a hospital has to work with other firms or departments. At higher tiers, priorities have to be made between widely divergent forms of health care, over large and varied geographical areas, so that scarce resources can be used in a proper priority setting. A case is therefore made out for complex machinery in terms of the need for equally complex allocative procedures.

Our argument would suggest that even if the number of tiers can be defended on operational grounds, they are not true levels because the input of values to each is not sufficiently distinct. There are clearly different levels representing the functions of the individual doctor and his basic unit: but beyond that the next point of real demarcation seems to be with the central authorities. The intermediate range of district, area and regional authorities are either properly subsumed under the central level, performing certain central functions by delegation, or are a conglomerate of institutions. In other words, we would assert that there are no distinct inputs of social values at the regional, area or district tiers.

This enfolding of several organizational tiers within a single systemic level may occur in other complex systems. Our concern is not with the enumeration of such tiers for its own sake, but with remarking the intuition of many practitioners that there are too many of them, and determining the reasons for this feeling. Where organizational tiers are not associated with the differentiation of value inputs, the allocations of authority and power give a sense of dysfunctional elaboration.[3]

If we then ask what are the relationships between the different systemic levels themselves, we find many similarities between hospital medicine and higher education. Multiple objectives are set by different groups at different levels of a complex health system. All have strong political or professional legitimacy. The centre is primarily concerned to produce an equitable, efficient and competent health service for the whole population. Those national criteria, based as they are on social and economic considerations, are not reflected in the norms of practitioners, whose primary concerns are with caring for individual patients and developing their standards of practice so as to earn the respect of their fellow professionals. The units within the hospitals are concerned to set high standards within their particular specialty, and consider themselves answerable for the quite specific groups of patients who come under their care. These specialist and professional norms are not easily reconcilable with those of the planners at the centre or within the regional health authorities, who have to respond to the need to redistribute resources from centres of declining population to the burgeoning new towns, and to reallocate resources from specialist and highly technological hospitals towards community medicine. There are, therefore, serious tensions between the different levels of a system in which facilities are both costly and scarce and in which (more so than in higher education) the freedom of individuals to act is constrained by resource allocations made for specific purposes. These circumstances give rise to negotiations similar to those which take place in higher education, though somewhat more control over priority setting is accepted because patients' needs are more pressing and more difficult to ignore than are the demands of higher education's clientele.

Schools
A secondary school teacher works within the following tiers: the individual; department, year or house; the school (but some schools have yet further intermediate tiers such as faculties or groups); the local authority (but some authorities have divisions and even, in London, a 'quartile' above the division); and the central authority. At minimum, there are thus five tiers; a larger school in London might be part of a range of as many as eight.

   In terms of our analysis there are probably no more than four systemic levels. But the schools also demonstrate that the number of levels can change. Such change is a result of changing assumptions about the number of points at which distinct values should be injected. To put it baldly, school teaching used to be determined by the head and by the local authority: but there are now many more groups competing for a share in the allocation of values from many different standpoints.

For purposes of allocations, resources and tasks, secondary schools may be divided into departments for academic work, or pastoral groupings such as houses or years. But schools, unlike universities, are convergent institutions. Adolescents must not be treated ambiguously. So in many cases the school, within the local authority, has two levels, in which the individual teacher and the head of the school are the main norm-setters.[4] It could be argued, however, that in a minority of schools the departments and the pastoral systems also make a distinctive normative input and thus constitute an additional level within the structure.

Where there are three rather than two levels within a school, we should expect to see distinctive work patterns based on distinctive curricular and pastoral assumptions at all three levels. That would be a matter of school or practitioner choice. It would mean that the head and the school had agreed that norm-setting in the curriculum and in the counselling, disciplinary and pastoral functions could develop within smaller groups than the whole school as represented by the head.

At the next level, of the relationship between local authorities and the schools, we need to establish that there are identifiable values which can be associated with the local authority itself. The local authority enables government to be nearer the governed, on the grounds that there are patterns of life and work which cannot be respected if services affecting individuals are administered centrally. Local government is also justified in terms of giving opportunities for more people to participate in the act of governing. These are, however, value statements about the importance of democracy and participation: they do not, in themselves, cope with issues which are intrinsically educational. As in the case of the higher education institutions, therefore, we may find the local authority to be concerned with a fiduciary role, and with the maintenance of a system which can take a fair view as between education and other competing demands on the ratepayer's resources and loyalties. This in its turn may give rise to demands for more participation by clients at the school level, where the curriculum is made and administered. Yet when parents or the public concerned with a particular school become dissatisfied with the way in which teachers are taking account of their wishes, the local authority may have to intervene on issues usually left to the basic unit or individual. It then becomes concerned with more than simply running the system, and is put in the position of having to make quality judgements. The potential for conflict over the determination of educational values was most prominently brought out by the case of William Tyndale School,[5] when the relationship between the local authority, the teachers and the governing body came under public scrutiny. The issues were not allocative but deeply normative issues related to the social values inculcated by education.

This brings us to reflect more generally on the relationships between central and local authorities and the schools. The schools themselves are allowed to determine their curriculum, on the assumption that teachers produce good learning as a product of their relationship with pupils and by working in such collegial settings as departments or year-groups. The situation is in that respect similar to the one depicted for higher education in our model. But the central authority has recently declared its interest in monitoring of standards, and — to judge by the terms of the Green Paper[6] — at least in part in ensuring that the schools meet social and economic needs. The possible consequences of such attempts might be estimated by transferring some of the characteristics of higher education to the secondary sector. If the central authority made judgements on such issues as the common core of the curriculum, it would need to push through those normative judgements in allocative and other operational decisions. Consideration of our model makes it dubious whether allocative decisions, or other operational uses of the centre's authority, would significantly affect the norms which are created and regulated in the schools. Decisions such as those about what form of assessment to impose would be more likely to change the normative pattern — as, indeed, the successive changes in secondary school examinations clearly illustrate. In practice, however, the British central authorities have not so far attempted to impose assessment or evaluation of any particular kind.

Social Work

Issues concerning the number of levels also arise in social work. A social worker concerned with a general caseload operates within a team, of which there might be several within an area. The area forms part of a fieldwork directorate. Fieldwork is part of the social services department. The social services department is then part of the larger local authority which may cater for education, environmental health, housing and planning, and other services. The social worker is thus within a seven-tier structure, if we add the central authority as well.

As with the health service, each tier can be described in terms of its allocative tasks, but there may not always be sufficient normative differentiation between tiers for there to be a true difference of level. It is difficult then to see precisely how or where the practitioner's norms are being tested and regulated by the values that are being set at other levels. Is the crucial element the team (or firm or department), or the area (hospital or other unit), or the fieldwork directorate (district management team), or social services department (area health authority), or total local authority (regional health authority), or central government?

The resulting relationships between different tiers may reflect these uncertainties. The individual professional worker feels that his prime responsibility is to the individual client or to quite small groups of clients. In performing his professional task, he develops judgements derived from his relationships with clients, as well as from a desire to achieve personal job satisfaction. Subscription to the group norms, within an area team, also conditions the way in which individual social workers act. At the same time, however, much of the work entails questions of value which are the concern of other levels of the system whose perspectives are different. Social work is controlled by local authorities whose members may have strong views about the allocation of resources for the treatment of the mentally ill, the old, the indigent or the deviant. In terms of our model, it is easy to see how norms that are created within the civic political environment can come into conflict with the views of the basic units and the individuals working within them. A different perspective again can be discerned at the level of the central government.

The Central Authorities and their Links with the System

We now turn to explore the applicability to our three chosen areas of some of the characteristics of central authorities, basic units and individuals which we have identified in higher education. All three examples rest on generalizations that apply to any system offering a service to individual clients through the work of individual professionals. Such a service cannot hope to create overall policies by simply adding together what they know about the work of the basic units. Nor can those responsible for the whole system expect to transfer global policies to local situations on the assumption that what seems workable at the centre will be acceptable and workable within the basic units. Certain types of system might be able to — and indeed, need to — assume compatibility of norms between the centre and the basic units. The armed services and the national railway system come to mind. But neither of these can afford to allow much pursuit of individual self-satisfaction, or dependence on peer norms, if reliable defence arrangements and efficient railroads are to result. They expect a uniform and specified output: they will contain a number of distinct tiers, but no clearly distinguishable levels. This is not true of higher education, nor of the other areas now under review.

Yet although each of the areas shares the characteristics which stem from the multiplicity of values legitimized at different levels, the three systems are organized differently. The differences are partly historical: for example, hospital doctors have strenuously resisted all past attempts to make hospitals into a local authority service because, rightly or wrongly, they regard central government as more likely to preserve their freedom than local government. Although they work within a national health service which is in direct hierarchical relationship with a central authority, as individuals they are not managed, but negotiate resources and other determinants of their discretion. The universities in the UK are, formally, at least, free charter institutions who receive grants directly from the central authorities. The grants are not, however, unconditional but are also the results of negotiation. School teaching, public sector higher education and social work are under the control of local authorities which themselves have an ambiguous authority relationship with the centre.

The modes of control are not explicitly differentiated in practice and differences in operation are sometimes more formal than real. But the different kinds of relationship embody assumptions about different degrees of control that the central authorities ought to maintain. Grants to publicly funded but independent institutions, such as those dependent on the Arts Council or the UGC, imply that government wants functions performed but leaves specific judgements to peer groups. The hierarchical structure of the NHS rests on the view that standards of health care should be indivisible, that hospital medicine is expensive, that its technology is explicit, that allocations can be rigorously tied to demonstrable need: but that individual practitioners can act with full discretion within such a framework. The local authority system, which includes part of higher education, is justified by the claim that there are judgements of quality, style and practice which should be closely informed by local considerations. The principles of that doctrine are rarely challenged, but the difficulty of determining what is appropriately a local decision can be seen in the tugs of war over such policies as the reorganization of secondary schools and the sale of council houses.

A full analysis of differences in systemic structure would have to be conducted in terms of the degrees of social control thought desirable, the technologies and scales of resources used, the characteristics of the client groups, and the underlying professional values. In practice, however, all the public services which depend on professional expertise seem to regress in different degrees towards a general mean in which central authorities, with or without local authorities sharing their role, control structures and resources in such a way as to ensure that social desiderata are met, but leave the norm-setting as it affects practice to basic units and individuals.

Basic Units in the Normative Mode

We now turn to look at the categories in terms of which basic units might usefully be described, based on the analysis set out in Chapter 6.

The first analytic category relates to the research–technology–scholarship triangle. The second concerns degrees of permeability, and of cohesiveness or separateness, of the curriculum. The third delineates the positivistic–relativistic axis. Each of these distinctions cuts into the substantive content of higher education and explores the ways in which the properties of the curriculum, as perceived by those concerned, affect the relationships between activities and those performing them.

Analogies to the Triangle and Permeabilities
As we noted in Chapter 6, different activities within higher education respond to different criteria: namely, usefulness and application (technology); the demonstrated mastery of a system of thought (scholarship); and the advancement of knowledge within the field (research). Responsiveness, intellectual mastery and creative development are, it might be argued, values which can be generally applied to any area of practitioner activity.

Each of these ascriptions can be thought of as ways of typifying the differing norms of the individual practitioner, for whom the basic unit provides both protection and a reference group. Each also specifies the practitioner's job satisfaction in terms of likely responses from some assumed audience of peers or clients or other respondents. Each carries with it different organizational implications.

Hospital doctors and the basic units within which they work display a wide diversity of orientations. All of them ultimately care for individual patients, in the same way as higher education can be said to care for learning. However, the nature of the job satisfaction will vary between, say, a pathologist (who may never see a patient except in certain control procedures, and whose norms are those of science, rigorously controlled in both application and research) and a geriatrician, psychiatrist or physical medicine specialist (whose successes are most likely to be achieved in the direct application of knowledge to patient care). There is a spectrum of power attributes and a range of different structures between those working on trials for a new drug, those concerned with basic molecular biological research and those involved in the development of prosthetic orthopaedics, or aural fenestration, or new social procedures in mental health. Those practitioners concerned with advancing knowledge and those

concerned with developing better techniques of care necessarily give rise to different specialisations and distinct peer-
group networks and basic units systems.

Analogies can be found in social work in such disparate
contexts as residential settings for the old, the deviant or
the otherwise vulnerable, or in field situations where social
workers encounter cases calling for individual casework, or
work with families or groups of young people (in intermediate treatment, for example) or with the community.
The underlying satisfactions from each working mode are
different. One tradition derives from socioanalytic techniques, in which the reference point is always the individual
client. Another might look to a political model of interactive and controlled conflict, regarding social work as a
means of redistributing power and resources. Another, again,
works within a frame of reference set by the control systems
administered by the courts, as through mental health legislation. All social workers to some extent work within all
three traditions, but their emphases differ. The lack of clarity
is one explanation for their uncertain status as a profession.

As already noted, secondary school teaching has a clearer
divide, created by the academic and pastoral functions of the
school.[7] Teachers may have the opportunity to choose
between quite different skills, although they are expected to
be careful to avoid artificial dichotomies between the educational and the social experiences of their pupils. Most teachers
engage in both sets of functions, though different kinds of
expertise are undoubtedly built up.

The function of creating, administering and testing the
curriculum involves reference not only to the standards set
internally but also to the world of textbooks and examinations. However, because the invisible college is less well
defined than in higher education, the peer group is generally
internal. In contrast, the pastoral functions of caring for the
personal and social problems of pupils, of offering guidance
and counsel (though these might be specialized tasks) and
of administering discipline bring some teachers into different
networks, operating on different assumptions, of social
workers, educational welfare officers, educational psychologists, child guidance clinics and the police. The dichotomies
are liable to be institutionalized. The academic approach

tends to be fairly well contained within the school; the pastoral involves crossing institutional boundaries and developing a specialized knowledge of how to do it.

Positivism and Relativism

Positivistic and relativistic traditions are reflected in attitudes towards clients resulting from the type of knowledge and skills which professionals possess. In higher education the positivistic approach affirms the importance of proven results and the existence of a clear body of subject matter. The relativistic approach puts an emphasis on judgement, on encouraging students to apply methods, on providing material that provides the raw material for, rather than the finished product of, the learning process.

In medicine[8] there is a well-remarked positivistic approach. It relies on a strong edifice of biological science upon which doctors feel competent to prescribe to their clients. But different concepts of bio-medical functions underlie different specialties in hospital medicine. Relativistic attitudes are required to take account of the social and familial role in health. They emphasize the importance of self-care and regard the patient as an agent of his own health, in which doctors take the role of providing specialist resources to a prime agent in the process. The policy consequences of the positivist–relativist distinction are enormous. Relativist concerns underlie the move from hospitals to community and family care in many areas of health where long stays in hospitals have hitherto been usual. They place an emphasis on preventative measures such as screening and health education, and argue against exclusive dependence on clinical intervention. They raise the issues of specialization and the relationships between doctors and the other health professions.

In social work, an advocate of the positivistic approach might argue in favour of the control of the client for his own good, starting with notions of dependency from which a client must be weaned. In contrast, a social worker adopting the relativistic approach would confront the client with the need for a contract specifying the roles of both parties and elaborating a reciprocal relationship between them. Such an approach postulates the development of familial independence and a reliance on community resources, of which the client's own efforts are a major component.

In schools, the positivistic and relativistic attitudes are comparable with those of higher education. The positivistic approach emphasizes the role of the teacher in promoting cognitive development. It assumes that there is a tradition of knowledge and skills to pass on. The relativistic approach relies on interaction between teachers and taught to define curricular content and allows for adaptation in response to the changing circumstances of society and the environment in general.

The Individual and Satisfaction of Personal Objectives
Individual practitioners claim to work for the good of their clients — the altruistic motive identified as an element of professionalism — but also, we have said, for the self-satisfaction expressed in the desire to secure and maintain a good individual reputation. Judgements of reputation are usually made in terms of the norms of basic units to which we have referred above.

Yet, as with higher education, the problems of boundaries and the possibility of secession (see Chapter 7) occur. In practice, however, the individual in higher education, whilst most usually contained within his developing but stable disciplinary tradition, has a larger margin for departure from received patterns of scholarship, research or technology than does a practitioner who is expected to give the services deemed essential in social work, teaching or medicine. Teachers may look for new patterns of curriculum and its organization but cannot move too easily without carrying a whole institution with them. Hospital doctors work within traditions of cumulative knowledge where certainty and control of applications are the boundaries within which inventiveness and creative change must be contained. Social workers are less constrained because their technology is uncertain and they have greater choice of their site and methods of work. Hence the fast flow of new forms of work — individual casework, group work, community work, intermediate treatment. In all these areas, authorized secession of the type associated with a Leavis or an Einstein is rare. Illich (in education) or Laing or even Freud (in psychiatry) have been regarded as deviant rather than as advancing new frontiers behind which socially reliable practitioners can readily be found. Invisible colleges of the kind to which higher education's practitioners belong are less powerful when institutional convergence is deemed to be important.

Individuality of practitioners, however, is a powerful force for change even if authorization is eventually required. The more heterogeneous the individuals within a basic unit and an institution, the larger the chances of conflict. The individual works within different degrees of prescription laid down in policies, but derives power from the fact that he is the practitioner exercising skills in essential processes, while the system imposes boundaries derived from somewhat more abstract realities.

The obligation to teach, while rewards paradoxically go for research, noted in the higher education teacher, has no exact parallel in the other examples. The medical specialists derive satisfaction from their work with patients. The policies within which social workers operate, and the mode and style of schooling, derive predominantly from practice. Practitioners select and order priorities, and the systems most often grant power to practice by sanctioning policies that develop incrementally. This happens, of course, in higher education as well. Academic drift in the polytechnics is a prime example of practitioner power working against, and successfully modifying, the declared aims of the system.

Styles of Evaluation
The relationships between different levels, as expressed in the normative and operational modes, have been typified in this book as being respectively those of evaluation and accountability, and the allocation of resources and tasks. Evaluation involves the making of judgements; accountability calls for the transmutation of those judgements into managerial or other control criteria by which individuals or institutions might be held to account. In its full sense within an employment system, accountability usually means being subject to another for the quality of work.

The classification of evaluative styles as instrumental, interactive or individualistic is useful in exposing the multiple assumptions that underlie the different areas of public policy. As we attempt to identify predominant approaches to evaluation in our sample areas, we become conscious of the ways in which complex institutions are shot through with different methods of control and of the making of judgements.

This becomes obvious when we consider the evaluation of hospital medicine. As we have noted, a hospital consultant is a member of a non-hierarchical collegium, lodged, paradoxically, within a complex organizational system which is largely hierarchical. Those elements which are hierarchically managed – the system for maintaining region, area, district, hospital or other units – are judged by instrumental criteria: how long do patients stay, what are the morbidity or mortality rates as between one part of the country or another, how much is spent on food in psychiatric hospitals as against acute medical units, and even what is the cost benefit of dying' as applied to renal dialysis or other high-cost procedures? Such instrumental evaluations form one of the bases of the monitoring activities which those in charge of the system are expected to undertake.

In contrast, the individual consultant is only subject to any evaluation when there is a disaster, when negligence is suspected or when he is seeking advancement. When judgements as to blame or innocence are made the consultant is evaluated in much the same way as is the higher education teacher – that is, interactively by his peers. It is by such procedures, too, that appointments to consultant positions are filled, merit awards are given and elections to the coveted Royal College fellowships are made.

Within the national health service, public inquiries are largely confined to specific incidents or series of incidents. Their style is unequivocally individualistic. The particularities of place and person are brought out and often exigently described before a judgement is made. Here, it seems, lies a contradiction. Institutions are evaluated as homogeneous lumps until serious public concern is felt. Then it is conceded that they can hold truths that lie too deep for measurement. When political or moral nerves are touched, the reasoning behind individual and group behaviour is brought into the open and the grosser outcomes of instrumental evaluation are no longer found relevant.

The central authorities do not evaluate social work provision on any systematic basis, although their advisers may review local authorities' development plans. The central authorities may also collate information on such matters as the number of qualified social workers employed by different local authorities — which could affect requests to the higher education sector for the development of more or fewer places on courses — or the provision of accommodation for various client groups, or the extent to which the housebound have telephones. Research and intelligence units within local authorities may also concern themselves with evaluation of a more or less instrumental kind. As with hospital medicine, judgements of quality are driven by egalitarian considerations.

At the working level, most evaluations are made personally by a supervisor on his or her subordinates, following the social work ethic, that relationship is interactive rather than instrumental. Social work supervision is also concerned with assessing how well the individual social worker is using his own skills in relationship to individual clients while working within such 'objective' considerations as the competing demands set up by untreated cases.[10]

A variety of complications arises from the particularly important role in social work of the politician. Perhaps more than in any public service, social workers are vulnerable to evaluations made outside their peer group. Politicians have views about the way that delinquent children should be treated, or the quality of the social services department's relationship with the family, or the nature of the social worker's relationships with the law and the courts. Some local authorities attempt systematic evaluations of outcomes; in others the elected members' policies or prejudices determine the nature of the assessments made, and the extent of the resources allocated.

Although there is a strong public tradition of performance assessment in the work of HM inspectors of schools, such assessment is interactive rather than instrumental in its values and tends to be presented in the context of an advisory service rather than a prescriptive force. The question of the definable objectives of education is seldom, however, far away. The creation of the Assessment of Performance Unit, the attempt at an elaboration of a core curriculum, and the associated evaluation procedures adumbrated in the Green Paper, no matter how well guarded against intentions of prescription, point to an element of instrumental concern.

One indirect but potent form of instrumental evaluation is achieved through the mechanism of external public examinations. Schools are liable to be judged, in popular esteem if not managerially, by the number and quality of GCE and CSE passes or by the admissions gained to universities. However, no local authority has yet made attempts along the lines of some American school districts to measure educational 'improvements' by blanket testing geared to the quantitative assessment of pre-specified learning gains.

Different levels in the school system tend to adopt different evaluative styles. As long as the centre accepts the view that schools should remain free to develop and operate their own curricula, this predicates an interactive style of evaluation. At the same time, there is a general political demand for more public knowledge about the results achieved by schools. It remains to be seen whether this instrumental requirement for the evaluation of performance will remain free of connection with allocations and other managerial pressures on individual institutions.

Local authority evaluation of schools and of teachers manifests a similar ambivalence of style and purpose. Teachers are certainly assessed: and such assessments affect their promotion prospects. Schools are assessed, and pressure can be exerted if standards and objectives are thought to be weak — even though the school's freedom to decide its own style and its own curriculum is respected within broad degrees of discretion. Within the school the structure is hierarchical, and the head is explicitly the manager. The school is expected to be convergent in its curriculum. Teachers are therefore required to create and teach to curricula that are sequential within disciplines and coherent across disciplines, so as to create a recognizable school style. But the mechanisms for the creation of the curriculum, and the administration of the pastoral tasks of the school, differ greatly.[11] Some schools are totally hierarchical. Others are collegial in style and infrastructure: the departments, or tutorial houses, or years, are peer groups collated by an academic board. The head and his senior colleagues may retain authority to modify or veto, but development is collegial within a management hierarchy.

Irrespective of the style of assessment, there is an enforced instrumentalism about school teaching. The show has to go on. Results must be achieved in an ordered environment. The gifted teacher will gain respect for his or her talents, but the main rewards will go to those who can run complicated structures, albeit in a caring and creative way. And the evaluations of structures are, by their very nature, likely to be based on clearly defined and publicly visible criteria.

Many parents (and, for that matter, many teachers) expect teaching to be judged on outcomes rather than on teachers' intentions. Yet the declared wisdom of British education has been towards interactive rather than instrumental relationships. The tension between these two modes is a characteristic feature of services in which the individual professional is expected to exercise considerable discretion within the public gaze.

School teachers and social workers may generate flourishing professional networks but neither of these highly interpersonal trades create visible products comparable with the clinical technique or the learned book which can establish a public reputation through the process of peer review. Such occupational characteristics condition the means by which evaluation can take place.

We have here described examples of the three evaluative styles as they seem to predominate in our sample areas. Yet examples of all of them could be found on closer examination of any zone of public activity. The generalization which we have substantiated is that evaluative technique and style are not neutral. They are determined as much by the purposes of the evaluation and the balance between information and prescription intended by the evaluator as by the technical substance of what is being evaluated.

Patterns of Accountability
The issue of accountability has been sharply posed in relation to both schools and the national health service. As yet, the theme has not been generalized in its application to social work, but the underlying problems have been, if anything, more acute in a field which seems permanently prone to outside inquiries on individual and institutional performance

— the best-known example of which is perhaps the case of Maria Colwell.[12]

Some individual cases imply that demands for stronger accountability in education have increased over the last few years. The William Tyndale Inquiry[13] established the duty of local authorities to assert publicly endorsed standards against the ideologies of particular teachers. In the county of Avon, the director of education resigned because he was compelled to subordinate the education department and the schools to corporate management systems. In Kent, examination successes are published by the local authority as a means of making schools more sensitive to parental evaluation and the moves towards a voucher system are intended to make the schools subject to the market mode of accountability. The Taylor Report on the government of schools[14] recommended that governors should set objectives and assess performance. The system as a whole has not followed these examples and evaluation from the centre is not associated with prescriptive assessment. But the conventional wisdom that teachers will determine and establish their own performance criteria is plainly under challenge.

In the NHS accountability has become a recurrent theme since the inflow of management thinking in the late 1960s.[15] It featured prominently in the guidance documents associated with the reorganization of the system as a whole; it has been implicit in several reports of inquiries into particular events where negligence or misconduct have been alleged. Indeed, the issues of accountability and evaluation are not as clamant in higher education as in areas where clients are less voluntary and activities are held to be more socially necessary — and where public concern about performance and value for money is, in consequence, more acute.

Words such as 'autonomous' are used, not altogether accurately, of hospital doctors. Their work is perhaps better described in terms of discretion and freedom. No consultant is, however, accountable to a management hierarchy in the way that other professions within the health services are. To say that the consultant is accountable at all is to use a broad sense of the term. In cases of negligence he can be pursued either by his employers (the regions); or through the courts for damages; or, in the case of serious misconduct, through the peer group represented by the professional licensing body. As we have already remarked, professional evaluations are made by the peer group at particular times for particular purposes. These, too, flow into accountability in terms of the reputation gained, the resources allowed and the advancement sanctioned. But they are generalized and cumulative and do not amount to a managerial scrutiny of performance.

Hospital medicine has its accountability systems but also a parallel system for review and complaint through the community health councils and the health service commissioners. These recent elaborations reflect the demand that the freedom of individual practitioners will be more strongly conditioned by clients' or patients' perceptions of need, and the impact that services make on them. The health service commissioner's style is primarily interactive in that he must judge each case on its merits by broad criteria of due process and equity. So, too, are the evaluations of CHCs, because their expression of the patients' point of view and their reviewing of performance is a matter of establishing impact. When CHCs act individualistically, on specific behaviour of individuals, they are thought to be acting unsatisfactorily, rather than determining precise outputs or outcomes. So far these essentially evaluative systems have produced no changes in the patterns of accountability but, as with the schools, the norms have been subject to considerable change.

Resource Allocations
Allocations are a principal means through which central authorities and institutions control and develop systems. They are made according to different underlying criteria in the normative mode.

In medicine, for example, allocations by central authorities are not made, except in the case of medical education, through collegial procedures, but through a managerial system. The primary criterion is not that of excellence but of defining needs to be met. Even when resources are allocated by a medical committee at the institutional level, the main criteria are the perceived needs of patients and the changing technologies that will meet them. Central authorities have on occasion sought to equalize provision by quite drastic reallocations of resources, in a way which must inevitably disturb the continuity and security of well-established units. Central allocative decisions are closely sensitive to social trends. For example, orthopaedics, and the resources that it attracts, has responded to such diverse influences as the onset of poliomyelitis; the discovery of remedial vaccines; and the varying popularity of motorcycles. Psychiatry has changed as opinion has shifted about the efficacy and acceptability of institutional therapies; but also in consequence of the development of drugs which have dramatically affected the balance between numbers of inpatients and outpatients. Such trends are relatively easy to note and act on. Longer-term developments in social thinking — such as the recurrent tensions between social, community and preventive medicine on the one side, and the application of technological hospital-based treatment on the other — may also, though more indirectly, affect allocations. For the most part, the promotion of equality is the norm that the central health authorities observe. The institutions, within district and area management, are sensitive to the pattern of health needs of their client groups. The basic units are, perhaps, most responsive to changing technology as well as to the overriding priority of treatment of individual patients.

While individual consultants share the freedom of work style enjoyed by higher education teachers, the overall allocations in hospital medicine are not made on the judgements of peer review against a background of social and economic criteria, as are the allocations made by academics working through the UGC. Instead, they are almost wholly determined by the centre out of its own sense of what is needed.

In the local authority services, of schools and social work, the central authorities make allocations through grant formulae that are explicitly concerned with meeting needs and inducing equality throughout the system. The requirement to meet needs equitably also determines allocations within the institutions, although some development of potential client demand is attempted when resources so allow.

Conclusions
In making these comparisons, we have chosen areas of

activity which are sufficiently similar for useful comparisons to be marked and also sufficiently different for informative contrasts to be drawn. We have not pursued all of the analogies that might have been derived from the first nine chapters of the book — for example, our discussion of innovation in systems in Chapter 8. We believe that such classifications as those relating to changes which are inexorable or coercive (and which impinge mainly in the operational mode), or changes which are radical or evolutionary (and depend mainly on the normative mode), are equally capable of being adapted to other areas of public policy and institutional life.

The reader who wishes to apply our model elsewhere could do so by developing more fully the sequence that we have sketched out in this chapter. Our model depends upon a clear distinction between norms and operations. The analyst, having marked this difference, should then go on to distinguish the systemic levels from organizational tiers in terms of whether there are distinctive value inputs to justify functions. He would then need to make a detailed study of the precise characteristics, both normative and operational, of the different levels of the system in question. That would lead to an exploration of the styles of evaluation and how they are derived from which value stances. The analysis must then examine what characteristics mark the norm-setting in each level of the system and what accountability, for what purposes, is correspondingly exacted. As a result of analysing the patterns of evaluation and accountability, the criteria underlying allocative practices can be identified. Finally, the motives and conditions of innovation become clearer once norms and operations are typified and the equilibria between them mapped out.

In suggesting this general analytic framework for the discussion of public systems which potently affect the welfare of individuals in society, we have sought to contribute towards the advancement of social policy studies. We hope that our attempt to demonstrate how complexity and variety can better be understood through analytic techniques will assist those who manage systems, and those who wish to find a credible basis for constructive criticism of them.

Notes

CHAPTER 1   Introduction

1   For example, P. Hall, H. Land, R.A. Parker and A. Webb, *Change, Choice and Conflict in Social Policy* (Heinemann, 1975); and R. A. Pinker, *Social Policy and Social Theory* (Heinemann, 1971).

2   T. Burns, *The BBC: Public Institution and Private World* (Macmillan, 1977).

CHAPTER 2   A Model for Higher Education

1   In ascribing these functions to central authorities we are deliberately telescoping the roles of the Department of Education and Science with respect to universities, and the local education authorities in England and Wales with respect to polytechnics and colleges (the position of the central institutions being different in Scotland). The local education authorities, in our use of the term, are 'central' in so far as they take on a number of the functions we attribute to the central level in our model. This ruling gives rise to questions to which we return in Chapters 4, 8 and 10, about the responsibilities of local government in relation to institutions which are partly national and partly local in character. But in any event, it should be noted that in the maintained sector of higher education, the allocation of capital resources and the approval of new developments are primarily a matter for the DES, even if recurrent funds are at the disposition of city or county hall.

2   It is in one sense an oversimplification to describe higher education in the USA as lacking a central component. Although the federal government has only a marginal role, some of the larger state networks – such as those of California and New York – can be seen as complete systems in themselves, with the state legislature functioning as the central authority. Taking the nation as a whole, however, there is no unitary system. In particular, the numerous private universities and colleges are answerable only to their individual governing bodies.

CHAPTER 3   The Development of Higher Education:
Changing Purposes Since 1945

1 A. H. Halsey, 'Quality and authority in British universities', *Times Higher Education Supplement*, 1 November 1964. In 1964, two-thirds of university teachers asked in a survey thought that 'more would mean worse'. That figure was reduced to 46 per cent in a survey conducted in 1974.

2 For example, University Grants Committee, *University Development, 1935–1947*, particularly p. 81.

3 For an entirely different interpretation see Tapper and Salter who assert that an elite structure became fragmented when the binary system was created in 1965. At that point the elite who were responsible for sustaining class dominance divided between those who wanted to sustain humanistic universities and those who wanted to advance vocationalism. Ted Tapper and Brian Salter, *Education and the Political Order* (Macmillan, 1978).

4 *University Development, 1935–1947*, p. 6.

5 ibid., p. 26.

6 *Report of the Committee on Scientific Manpower*, May 1946.

7 *University Development, 1935–1947*, p. 29.

8 ibid., p. 33.

9 ibid., p. 80.

10 ibid., p. 81.

11 UGC, *University Development, 1947–1952*, Cnd 8875, p. 12.

12 ibid., pp. 20–7.

13 UGC, *University Development, 1952–1957*, Cmnd 534.

14 ibid., p. 46.

15 The SSRC created a Research Initiatives Board in 1974 and made several public statements of its intention to support initiatives in research related to the improvement of public policy.

16 Sir John Wolfenden, Evidence to Committee of Public Accounts, *Parliament and Control of University Expenditure*, Session 1966/7, 290 (HMSO, 1 December 1966).

17 UGC, *University Development, 1962–1967*, Cmnd 3820, p. 49.

18 ibid., p. 80.

19 *Higher Education*, Report of the Committee appointed by the Prime Minister under the chairmanship of Lord Robbins, 1961–3, Cmnd 2154 (HMSO, 1963).

20 *A Plan for Polytechnics and Other Colleges*, Cmnd 300 (HMSO, 1965).

21 Following the principles laid down in the Houghton Committee Report, *Report of the Committee of Inquiry into the Pay of Non-University Teachers*, Cmnd 5848, 1974), para. 162: 'We feel strongly that teachers doing work which is similar to that being done in universities should as a matter of principle be paid broadly comparable rates to their university counterparts and should have broadly similar career prospects.' From January 1975 until October 1979 polytechnic salaries were in advance of those of university teachers.

22 G. J. Giles, 'The rise of the polytechnics in Britain', International Conference, 'University Today', Dubrovnik, 1977 (unpublished).

23 T. Burgess and J. Pratt, *Polytechnics: A Report* (Pitman, 1974), *Education and the School* (Penguin, 1977).
24 M. C. Davis, 'The development of the CNAA. A study of a validating agency', PhD thesis, Loughborough University of Technology, 1979. Also 'Final report on SSRC project' deposited at British National Lending Library.
25 Ann Bone, in her contribution to 'Higher education and the state' (unpublished), describes how radical reforms were completed in Oxford and Cambridge in 1882 'initiated and imposed by the state but modified by the university . . . and carried out, if with reluctance, by consent'.
26 E. Ashby and M. Anderson, *Portrait of Haldane at Work on Education* (Archon Books, 1974).
27 UGC, *University Development, 1947–1952*, p. 8.
28 Ashby and Anderson, op. cit., pp. 45–7.
29 UGC, *University Development, 1935–1947*, p. 77.
30 *The National Plan*, Cmnd 2764 (HMSO, 1965).
31 UGC, *University Development, 1962–1967*, p. 131.
32 UGC, *Annual Survey 1975–76*, Cmnd 6758 (HMSO, 1977), pp. 9–15.
33 The universities refrain from advertising undergraduate courses, but no holds are barred in recruitment for graduate courses. Public sector institutions are not restrained by the same conventions.

CHAPTER 4 Planning and Decision-Making for the Whole System

1 *Higher Education*, Cmnd 2154 (HMSO, 1963), pp. 6–7.
2 M. Kogan, *Appraisal of country educational policy reviews* (document prepared for OECD, 1979).
3 Ministry of Education, *Higher Technological Education* (HMSO, 1945).
4 M. Kogan, *Educational Policy Making* (Allen & Unwin, 1975), pp. 203–16.
5 Where there is more than one central authority the divisions may follow general national assumptions about the structure of government rather than any pattern specially devised for higher education. For example, the Swedish central authorities divide between the Ministry of Education, responsible for overall policy, and the National Board of Colleges and Universities, responsible for the administration and planning of the system. But that distribution of functions is not between allocative and academic decision-making.
6 Personal communication from Dr Margaret Scotford Archer, 1978.
7 Don K. Price, *The Scientific Estate* (Harvard University Press, 1965).
8 Central Policy Review Staff, *A Framework for Government Research and Development*, Cmnd 4814 (the Rothschild Report) (HMSO, 1973).
9 Burton R. Clark, *Academic Co-ordination* (Yale Higher Education Research Group, Working Paper no. 24, 1978).
10 R. O. Berdahl, *British Universities and the State* (University of California Press, 1959).

11 R. Premfors and B. Östergren, *Systems of Higher Education: Sweden* (International Council for Educational Development, 1978). See also J. -E. Lane, *Autonomy: A Theoretical Approach* (Center for Administrative Studies, Working Paper No. 5, Umea University, 1977).
12 E. Ashby and M. Anderson, *Portrait of Haldane at Work on Education* (Archon Books, 1974).
13 Clark, op. cit.
14 Recent changes in Sweden seem to have simultaneously weakened the power of the professors and of the centre by increasing community control. Only time will tell how far these changes will stick.
15 Department of Education and Science and the Scottish Education Department, *Higher Education into the 1990s, A Discussion Document* (HMSO, 1977).
16 Centre for Environmental Research and Innovation, *Alternative Educational Futures in the United States and in Europe: Methods, Issues and Policy Relevance* (OECD, 1972).

CHAPTER 5   The Institution

1 G. C. Moodie and R. Eustace, *Power and Authority in British Universities* (Allen & Unwin, 1974), particularly chs 3 and 4.
2 Burton R. Clark, *Academic Co-ordination* (Yale Higher Education Research Group, Working Paper 24, 1978).
3 J. V. Baldridge, D. V. Curtis, G. Ecker and G. L. Riley, *Policy Making and Effective Leadership* (Jossey-Bass, 1978).
4 M. D. Cohen and J. G. March, *Leadership and Ambiguity, The American College President* (McGraw-Hill, 1974). The literature from which these phrases are taken is well summarized in Baldridge *et al.*, op. cit.
5 We are indebted to Moodie and Eustace, op. cit., for many of the ideas discussed in this section.
6 T. Becher, J. F. Embling and M. Kogan, *Systems of Higher Education, United Kingdom* (International Council for Educational Development, 1978).
7 This was first discussed in *Power and Conflict in the University*, (Jossey-Bass, 1971), but has since been elaborated in Baldridge *et al.*, *Policy Making and Effective Leadership*, op. cit.
8 F. G. Bailey, *Morality and Expediency: The Folk Lore of Academic Politics* (Blackwell, 1977).
9 Becher, Embling and Kogan, op. cit.
10 Baldridge *et al.*, op. cit.
11 The place of student unions within this analysis should be noted. It is not clear whether they should be regarded as internal or external to the institution. A growing proportion of the functions of academic institutions can be seen to be shared by student unions. For example, a student union may call for resources to be diverted from particular forms of research and teaching so that its parent institution can take on a different relationship with a broader community of clients. In doing so, the union seeks to

establish an alternative system of norm-setting in which the institution becomes less dependent on the norms developed by individuals and basic units. Institutional assets, such as building and finance, have also become part of the domain over which negotiation between the institution and the student union can take place. Operational decisions reflect normative balances.

Student unions increasingly assert the right to provide services for students which the institution itself cannot or will not provide. Such provision is not always confined to recreational facilities: it may involve the unions in performing pastoral functions of the kind normally undertaken by the basic units or the institution as a whole. There can indeed be overt competition between the institution and the student union, to the point at which the latter takes on the role of a parallel or counter institution.

CHAPTER 6   Basic Units

1   A valuable overview of the functions of basic units is to be found in M. Trow, 'The American academic department as a context for learning', *Studies in Higher Education*, vol. 2, no. 2, March 1976.

2   See J. Platt, *Realities in Social Research: An Empirical Study of British Sociologists* (Sussex University Press, 1976), for a detailed analysis of this phenomenon in relation to social science.

3   This is partly a question of social, rather than academic, acceptability. Those entering higher education appear readily to pick up the current 'pecking order' of professions and semi-professions, and to frame their applications for courses in the light of such general appraisals. Hence, for example, the perennial complaints that some branches of engineering do not attract their fair share of able applicants, and the periodic attempts to improve their public esteem (particularly among science-based sixth-form teachers and pupils).

4   This derives from Basil Bernstein's useful analysis of the contrasts between 'strong' and 'weak' classification at the level of school curricula. See B. Bernstein, *Class, Codes and Control*, Vol. 3 (Routledge & Kegan Paul, 1975).

5   This similarly reflects Bernstein's account, in *Class, Codes and Control*, of school curricula which manifest a 'strong' (as opposed to 'weak') framing.

6   An illuminating case-study of one such course is given in G. C. Fisher, S. Kapur and J. E. C. McGarvey, 'Physics and chemistry for environmental scientists: the evaluation of a tertiary level science course', *Studies in Higher Education*, vol. 3, no. 2, October 1978.

7   See notes 4 and 5 above.

8   Looked at from a closer vantage point, even a medium-sized basic unit is likely to display much internal variety. Indeed, it is sometimes argued that academic departments (and presumably other comparable aggregations) ought deliberately to seek heterogeneity as a source of intellectual vigour. See, for example, D. Macrae, 'The departmental zoo', *New Society*, 13 November 1968.

CHAPTER 7   The Individual Level

1 A. H. Halsey and M. Trow, *The British Academics* (Faber, 1971).
2 An entertaining account of this process is given in Michael Thompson, 'Class, caste, the curriculum cycle and the cusp catastrophe', *Studies in Higher Education*, vol. 1, no. 1, March 1976.
3 The two classic accounts — the first of disciplines as real entities, the second of education as socially derived — are to be found respectively in Paul H. Hirst, *Knowledge and the Curriculum* (Routledge & Kegan Paul, 1974), and in Basil Bernstein, *Class, Codes and Control: Vol. 3: Towards a Theory of Educational Transmission* (Routledge & Kegan Paul, 1975).
4 Examples of this process are tellingly illustrated in the writings of T. S. Kuhn. See especially *The Copernican Revolution* (Harvard University Press, 1957); *The Structure of Scientific Revolutions* (University of Chicago Press, 1962); and *The Essential Tension* (University of Chicago Press, 1977).
5 This remains true of universities despite various efforts over the years to persuade them to take teaching competence into account: see specially the text of the agreement between the University Authorities Panel and the Association of University Teachers concerning the procedure and criteria to be used in connection with the probationary period, promulgated in 1974. As far as polytechnics and colleges are concerned, promotion has in the past tended to depend on a combination of seniority, leadership qualities and managerial competence: but given the growing emphasis on research in the 'non-autonomous' sector, the criteria there have begun more closely to resemble those of universities.
6 Eric Hewton *et al.*, *Supporting Teaching for a Change* (Nuffield Group for Research and Innovation in Higher Education, 1975).
7 Oxbridge dons can admittedly earn substantial teaching reputations. We would argue that this is because, as institutions enjoying unrivalled status, both Oxford and Cambridge can afford the luxury of carrying career teachers as well as career researchers — a luxury in which few other British universities apparently feel able to indulge.
8 J. Platt, *Realities of Social Research: An Empirical Study of British Sociologists* (Sussex University Press, 1976), offers a clear account of such contrasts in social science research.
9 *Higher Education into the 1990s* (HMSO, 1977).
10 J. S. Bruner, J. J. Goodnow and G. A. Austin, *A Study of Thinking* (Wiley, 1956); L. Hudson, *Contrary Imaginations* (Methuen, 1966); F. Marton and R. Saljo, 'On qualitative differences in learning', *British Journal of Educational Psychology*, vol. 46, 1976; G. Pask, 'Styles and strategies of learning', *British Journal of Educational Psychology*, vol. 46, 1976.
11 H. S. Becker, B. Greer and E. C. Hughes, *Making the Grade: The Academic Side of College Life* (Wiley, 1968); P. Marris, *The Experience of Higher Education* (Routledge & Kegan Paul, 1964); B. R. Snyder, *The Hidden Curriculum* (Knopf, 1971).

12   C. M. L. Miller and M. Parlett, *Up to the Mark* (Society for Research in Higher Education, 1974).

13   W. G. Perry Jnr, *Forms of Intellectual and Ethical Development in the College Years* (Holt, Rinehart & Winston, 1970).

14   J. Bliss and J. Ogborn, *Students' Reactions to Undergraduate Science* (Heinemann Educational for Nuffield Foundation, 1977); D. S. Zinberg, 'Education through science; the early stages of career development in chemistry', *Social Studies of Science*, vol. 6, 1976.

15   R. Challis, 'The experience of mature students', *Studies in Higher Education*, vol. 1, no. 2, October 1976.

16   M. Parlett *et al.*, *Learning from Learners* (Nuffield Group for Research and Innovation in Higher Education, 1976).

17   Snyder, op. cit.

CHAPTER 8   Initiating and Adapting to Change

1   K. Lewin, *Field Theory in Social Science: Selected Theoretical Papers* (Tavistock, 1952).

2   B. Östergren and B. Berg, *Innovations and Innovation Processes in Higher Education* (Swedish National Board of Universities and Colleges, 1977).

3   Asa Briggs, in D. Daiches (ed.), *The Idea of a New University* (Deutsch, 1964).

4   Nuffield Group for Research and Innovation in Higher Education, *Newsletter No. 7*, October 1976.

5   J. Whitburn, M. Mealing and C. Cox, *People in Polytechnics: A Survey of Polytechnic Staff and Students 1972–3* (Society for Research in Higher Education, 1976.

6   T. Burgess and J. Pratt, *Polytechnics: A Report* (Pitman, 1974); see also G. Neave, 'Academic drift: some views from Europe', *Studies in Higher Education*, vol. 3, no. 1, March 1978.

7   Judith Riley, 'Course teams at the Open University', *Studies in Higher Education*, vol. 4, no. 2, October 1979.

8   *Education: A Framework for Expansion*, Cmnd 5174 (HMSO, 1972).

9   D. Hencke, *Colleges in Crisis: The Reorganisation of Teacher Training, 1971–7* (Penguin, 1978).

10   University Grants Committee, Department of Education and Science, Scottish Education Department, *Audio-Visual Aids in Higher Scientific Education* (the Brynmor Jones Report) (HMSO, 1965).

11   A rare exception, in terms of a successful course based largely on video-taped material, is documented in N. Pronay, 'Towards independence in learning history', *Studies in Higher Education*, vol. 4, no. 1, March 1979.

12   R. Hooper, *The National Development Programme in Computer Assisted Learning: Final Report of the Director* (Council for Educational Technology, 1977).

13   See, for a review of the various strategies employed, E. Hewton,

et al., *Supporting Teaching for a Change* (Nuffield Group for Research and Innovation in Higher Education, 1975).

14 A good illustration is provided in S. Ashman and A. George, 'Course committees in the Polytechnic of North London', unpublished project report, MA in Curriculum Development in Higher Education, University of Sussex, 1977.

15 E. Ashby and M. Anderson, *The Rise of the Student Estate in Britain* (Macmillan, 1970).

16 T. S. Kuhn, *The Structure of Scientific Revolutions* (University of Chicago Press, 1962).

17 Nuffield Group for Research and Innovation in Higher Education, *The Drift of Change* (Nuffield Foundation, 1975).

18 Some cases are documented in B. Klug (ed.), *A Question of Degree* (Nuffield Group for Research and Innovation in Higher Education, 1976).

19 To give a negative illustration of this point, a sustained attempt by the Schools Council, over more than a decade, to introduce a somewhat less specialized sixth-form examination structure was strongly countered, and eventually defeated by the determination of tertiary institutions to maintain the existing pattern.

20 E. Hewton, 'A strategy for promoting curriculum development in universities', *Studies in Higher Education*, vol. 4, no. 1, March 1979.

CHAPTER 9   Evaluation, Accountability and the Allocation of Resources

1 T. Becher and S. Maclure (eds), *Accountability in Education* (N F E R Publishing for Social Science Research Council, 1978).

2 A fuller analysis can be found in T. Becher and S. Maclure, *The Politics of Curriculum Change* (Hutchinson, 1978).

3 Examples of the genre can be found in H. J. Butcher and E. Rudd (eds), *Contemporary Problems in Higher Education: An Account of Research* (McGraw-Hill, 1972); in N. J. Entwistle and J. D. Wilson, *Degrees of Excellence: The Academic Achievement Game* (Hodder & Stoughton, 1977); and in various issues of *Higher Education*.

4 See, for instance, M. Parlett and G. Dearden (eds), *Introduction to Illuminative Evaluation: Studies in Higher Education* (Pacific Soundings Press, 1977).

5 The case-study approach is illustrated in D. Hamilton, D. Jenkins, C. King, B. MacDonald and M. Parlett (eds), *Beyond the Numbers Game* (Macmillan, 1977).

6 An interesting sample is provided in Parlett and Dearden, op. cit., in the form of a commissioned evaluation of Wellesley College.

7 University of Birmingham, *Report of the Review Body Appointed by the Council of the University* (Grimond Report) (University of Birmingham, 1972).

8 'Report of the Syndicate on the Relationship Between the University and the Colleges' (chaired by Lord Bridges), *Cambridge University Reporter*, vol. XCII, no. 28, 13 March 1962.

9 University of Oxford, *Report of Commission of Enquiry* (the Franks Report), Vol. 1 (Oxford University Press, 1966).

10 B. MacDonald *et al.*, *Understanding Computer Assisted Learning* (McGraw-Hill, 1978).

11 R. O. Berdahl, *British Universities and the State* (University of California Press, 1959).

12 Such evaluations were proposed in National Board for Prices and Incomes Report No. 145, *Standing Reference on the Pay of University Teachers in Great Britain*, Cmnd 4334 (HMSO, 1970).

13 The relevant data were clearly set out in the Report of the Committee on Higher Education, *Higher Education*, Appendix Two (A), Cmnd 2154-II (HMSO, 1963), and subjected to a subsequent detailed critique in B. Klug, *The Grading Game* (NUS Publications, 1977).

14 For example, the first student prospectus on Manchester University courses (Nuffield Group for Research and Innovation in Higher Education, *Newsletter No. 5*, October 1974) was subsequently brought up to date and reprinted with a grant from central university funds.

15 See Burton R. Clark, *Academic Co-ordination* (Yale Higher Education Research Group, Working Paper no. 24, 1978), for a discussion of the 'Professorial Guild'.

16 A fuller account of the mechanisms of validation is set out in ch. 8 of T. Becher, J. Embling and M. Kogan, *Systems of Higher Education: The United Kingdom* (International Council for Educational Development 1978).

17 Committee of Public Accounts, Special Report, *Parliament and Control of University Expenditure*, Session 1966/7, 290 (HMSO, 1967).

18 R. Startup, 'Material resources and the academic role', *Studies in Higher Education*, vol. 4, no. 2, October 1979.

CHAPTER 10 Adapting the Model to other Social Policy Areas

1 The negotiative relationship is elaborated rigorously in Margaret Scotford Archer, *Social Origins of Educational Systems*, Sage Studies in Social and Educational Change, vol. 9 (Sage Publications, 1978).

2 A different approach, not necessarily in conflict with ours, is contained in the work of Elliott Jaques. See particularly *A General Theory of Bureaucracy* (Heinemann, 1976), Part III. Professor Jaques identifies levels on the basis of the time-span of discretion, and differentiations of human capacity.

3 Royal Commission on the National Health Service, M. Kogan *et al.*, *The Working of the National Health Service, Research Paper No. 1* (HMSO, 1978).

4 T. Packwood, 'The school as a hierarchy', *Educational Administration*, vol. 5, no. 2, Spring 1977.

5 Report of the William Tyndale Junior and Infants School Public Inquiry (the Auld Report) (ILEA, 1976).
6 *Education in Schools. A Consultative Document* (Green Paper), Cmnd 6869 (HMSO, 1977).
7 D. Johnson, M. Kogan *et al.*, *Secondary Schools and the Welfare Network* (Allen & Unwin, forthcoming).
8 Margaret Stacey, *Health and Health Policy: Priorities for Research*, Appendix III: Concepts of Health and Illness (SSRC, 1977).
9 A. J. Culyer, R. G. Lavers and Allan Williams, 'Health indicators', in Andrew Schonfield and Stella Shaw (eds), *Social Indicators and Social Policy* (Heinemann, 1972).
10 W. Reid and L. Epstein, *Task Centred Case Work* (Columbia University Press, 1972); W. Reid and A. Shyne, *Brief and Extended Case Work* (Columbia University Press, 1969); J. M. Hutton, *Short Term Contracts in Social Work* (Routledge & Kegan Paul, 1977).
11 Johnson *et al.*, op. cit.
12 Report of the Committee of Inquiry into the Care and Supervision Provided in Relationship to Maria Colwell (DHSS, 1974).
13 William Tyndale Inquiry (see note 5).
14 DES and Welsh Office, *A New Partnership for our Schools* (HMSO, 1977).
15 Royal Commission Report (see note 3), Field Interview Survey, Section 11.

Bibliography

This bibliography contains the works to which we refer in the text and other principal authorities we have consulted. It is not an attempt to give an exhaustive bibliography of the literature on British higher education, let alone that of other countries.

Journals

Higher Education, Elsevier.
The Higher Education Review, Cornmarket Press.
New Universities Quarterly, Blackwell.
Studies in Higher Education, Carfax.
Times Higher Education Supplement, Times Publications.

Series of publications

International Council for Educational Development, *Systems of Higher Education* (studies published in 1978 of *Australia, Canada, Federal Republic of Germany, France, Iran, Japan, Mexico, Poland, Sweden, Thailand, United Kingdom, United States*).
Publications of the Carnegie Commission on Higher Education (a large-scale series of studies, mainly, but not exclusively, about the USA).
OECD Country Reviews of Education. A series beginning in 1961, most items of which include reference to current policies and problems in higher education in the different countries.

Official reports (in date order)

University Grants Committee, *Annual Survey 1975–76*, Cmnd 6758 (HMSO, 1977).
University Grants Committee, *University Development* (reports):
  1935–1947.
  1947–1952, Cmnd 8875.
  1952–1957, Cmnd 534.
  1962–1967, Cmnd 3820.
Ministry of Education, *Higher Technological Education* (HMSO, 1945).
Report of the Committee on Scientific Manpower (the Barlow Report) (HMSO, May 1946).

DES, *A Plan for Polytechnics and Other Colleges*, Cmnd 300 (HMSO, 1965).
Report of the Committee Appointed by the Prime Minister under the chairmanship of Lord Robbins 1961–63, *Higher Education*, Cmnd 2154 (HMSO, 1963).
UGC, DES, Scottish Education Department, *Audio-Visual Aids in Higher Scientific Education* (the Brynmor Jones Report) (HMSO, 1965).
Committee of Public Accounts, (Wolfenden Committee), *Parliament and Control of University Expenditure*, Session 66/67, 290 (HMSO, 1 December 1966).
National Board for Prices and Incomes, Report No. 145, *Standing Reference on the Pay of University Teachers in Great Britain*, Cmnd 4334 (HMSO, 1970).
DES, *Education: A Framework for Expansion*, Cmnd 5174 (HMSO, 1972).
Central Policy Review Staff, *A Framework for Government Research and Development* (the Rothschild Report), Cmnd 4814 (HMSO, 1973).
Report of the Committee of Inquiry into the Pay of Non-University Teachers (the Houghton Committee), Cmnd 5848 (HMSO, 1974).
Report of the Committee of Inquiry into the Care and Supervision Provided in Relation to Maria Colwell (DHSS, 1974).
DES, *Education in Schools. A Consultative Document* (Green Paper), Cmnd 6869 (HMSO, 1977).
DES and Welsh Office, *A New Partnership for our Schools* (the Taylor Report) (HMSO, 1977).
DES, *Higher Education in the 1990s: A Discussion Document* (HMSO, 1977).
Royal Commission on the National Health Service, M. Kogan *et al.*, *The Working of the National Health Service, Research Paper No. 1* (HMSO, 1978).

Books and articles

Archer, M. S., *Social Origins of Educational Systems*, Sage Studies in Social and Educational Change, vol. 9 (Sage Publications, 1978).
Ashby, E., and Anderson, M., *Portrait of Haldane at Work on Education* (Archon Books, 1974).
Ashman, S., and George, A., 'Course committees in the Polytechnic of North London', unpublished project report, MA in Curriculum Development in Higher Education, University of Sussex, 1977.
Bailey, F. G., *Morality and Expediency: The Folk Lore of Academic Politics* (Blackwell, 1977).
Baldridge, J. V., *Power and Conflict in the University* (Jossey-Bass, 1971).
Baldridge, J. V., Curtis, D. V., Ecker, G., and Riley, G. L., *Policy Making and Effective Leadership* (Jossey-Bass, 1978).
Becher, T., Embling, J. F., and Kogan, M., *Systems of Higher Education:*

United Kingdom (International Council for Educational Development, 1978).

Becher, T., and Maclure, S., *The Politics of Curriculum Change* (Hutchinson, 1978).

Becher, T., and Maclure, S. (eds), *Accountability in Education* (NFER Publishing for SSRC, 1978).

Becker, H. S., Greer, B., and Hughes, E. C., *Making the Grade: The Academic Side of College Life* (Wiley, 1968).

Berdahl, R. O., *British Universities and the State* (University of California Press, 1959).

Bernstein, B., *Class, Codes and Control: Vol. 3, Towards a Theory of Educational Transmission* (Routledge & Kegan Paul, 1963).

Blau, P. M., and Scott, W. M., *Formal Organizations, A Comparative Approach* (Routledge & Kegan Paul, 1963).

Bliss, J., and Ogborn, J., *Students' Reactions to Undergraduate Science* (Heinemann Educational Books for Nuffield Foundation, 1977).

Bone, Ann, 'Higher Education and the schools', unpublished.

Bridges, Edward, 'Report of the Syndicate on the Relationship Between the University and the Colleges', *Cambridge University Reporter*, vol. XCII, no. 28, 13 March 1962.

Briggs, Asa, in Daiches, D. (ed), *The Idea of a New University* (Deutsch, 1964).

Bruner, J. S., Goodnow, J. J., and Austin, G. A., *A Study of Thinking* (Wiley, 1956).

Burgess, T., *Education and the School* (Penguin, 1977).

Burgess, T., *Planning for Higher Education*, Cornmarket Papers on Higher Education (Cornmarket Press, 1972).

Burgess, T., and Pratt, J., *Polytechnics: A Report* (Pitman, 1974).

Burns, T., *The BBC: Public Institution and Private World* (Macmillan, 1977).

Butcher, H. J., and Rudd, E. (eds), *Contemporary Problems in Higher Education: An Account of Research* (McGraw-Hill, 1972).

Centre for Educational Research and Innovation, *Alternative Educational Futures in the United States and in Europe: Methods, Issues and Policy Relevance* (OECD, 1972).

Challis, R., 'The experience of mature students', *Studies in Higher Education*, vol. 1, no. 2, October 1976.

Clark, Burton R., *Academic Co-ordination* (Yale Higher Education Research Group, Working Paper no. 24, 1978).

Clark, Burton R., *Problems of Access in the Content of Academic Structures* (Yale Higher Education Group, Working Paper no. 16, 1977).

Clark, Burton R., *Structures of Post-Secondary Education* (Yale Higher Education Group, Working Paper no. 10, 1978).

Clark, Burton R., *The Changing Relationships Between Higher Education and Government: Some Perspectives from Abroad* (Yale University Higher Education Research Group, Working Paper no. 21, 1977).

Cohen, M. D., and March, J. G., *Leadership and Ambiguity: The American College President* (McGraw-Hill, 1974).

Culyer, A. J., Lavers, R. G., and Williams, Allan, 'Health indicators', in Andrew Schonfield and Stella Shaw (eds), *Social Indicators and Social Policy* (Heinemann, 1972).

Daiches, D. (ed), *The Idea of a New University* (Deutsch, 1964).

Davis, M. C., 'The development of the CNAA: a study of a validating agency', PhD Thesis, Loughborough University of Technology, 1979. Also 'Final report on SSRC project' deposited at British National Lending Library.

Donaldson, L., *Policy and the Polytechnics* (Saxon House, 1975).

Entwistle, N. J., and Wilson, J. D., *Degrees of Excellence: The Academic Achievement Game* (Hodder & Stoughton, 1977).

Fielden, J., and Lockwood, G., *Planning and Management in Universities. A Study of British Universities* (Chatto & Windus, 1973).

Fisher, G. C., Kapur, S., and McGarvey, J. E. C., 'Physics and chemistry for environmental scientists: the evaluation of a tertiary level science course', *Studies in Higher Education*, vol. 3, no. 2, October 1978.

Franks, Oliver, the Franks Report; see under 'University of Oxford'.

Giles, G. J., 'The rise of the polytechnics in Britain', International Conference, 'University Today', Dubrovnik, 1977, unpublished.

Graaff, Van de, J., *The Structure of Academic Governance in Great Britain* (Yale Higher Education Programme, Working Paper no. 13, 1976).

Hajnal, J., *The Student Trap* (Penguin, 1972).

Hall, P., Land, H., Parker, R. A., and Webb, A., *Change, Choice and Conflict in Social Policy* (Heinemann, 1975).

Halsey, A. H., 'Quality and authority in British universities', *Times Higher Education Supplement*, 1 November 1964.

Halsey, A. H., and Trow, M., *The British Academics* (Faber, 1971).

Hamilton, D., Jenkins, D., King, C., MacDonald, B., and Parlett, M. (eds), *Beyond the Numbers Game* (Macmillan, 1977).

Hencke, D., *Colleges in Crisis: The Reorganisation of Teacher Training, 1971–7* (Penguin, 1978).

Hewton, E., 'A strategy for promoting curriculum development in universities', *Studies in Higher Education*, vol. 4, no. 1, March 1979.

Hewton, E., et al., *Supporting Teaching for a Change* (Nuffield Group for Research and Innovation in Higher Education, 1975).

Hirst, P. H., *Knowledge and the Curriculum* (Routledge & Kegan Paul, 1974).

Hooper, R., *The National Development Programme in Computer Assisted Learning: Final Report of the Director* (Council for Educational Technology, 1977).

Hudson, L., *Contrary Imaginations* (Methuen, 1966).

Hutton, J. M., *Short Term Contracts in Social Work* (Routledge & Kegan Paul, 1977).

Jaques, E., *A General Theory of Bureaucracy* (Heinemann, 1976).

Jevons, F. R., and Turner, H. D., *What Kind of Graduate Do We Need?* (Oxford University Press, 1973).

Johnson, D., Kogan, M., et al., *Secondary Schools and the Welfare Network* (Allen & Unwin, forthcoming).

Kogan, M., *Appraisal of Country Educational Policy Reviews* (document prepared for OECD, 1979).

Kogan, M., *Educational Policy Making* (Allen & Unwin, 1975).

Klug, B. (ed), *A Question of Degree* (Nuffield Group for Research and Innovation in Higher Education, 1976).

Klug, B., *The Grading Game* (NUS Publications, 1977).

Kuhn, T.S., *The Copernican Revolution* (Harvard University Press, 1957).

Kuhn, T. S., *The Structure of Scientific Revolutions* (University of Chicago Press, 1962).

Kuhn, T. S., *The Essential Tension* (University of Chicago Press, 1977).

Lane, J.-E., *Autonomy: A Theoretical Approach* (Center for Administrative Studies, Working Paper No. 5, Umea University, 1977).

Levy, D. C., *Universities and Governance: The Comparative Politics of Higher Education* (Yale Higher Education Research Group, Working Paper no. 31, 1978).

Lewin, K., *Field Theory in Social Science*, Selected Theoretical Papers (Tavistock, 1952).

MacDonald, B., *et al.*, *Understanding Computer Assisted Learning* (McGraw-Hill, 1978).

Macrae, D., 'The departmental zoo', *New Society*, 13 November 1968.

Marris, P., *The Experience of Higher Education* (Routledge & Kegan Paul, 1964).

Marton, F., and Saljo, R., 'On qualitative differences in learning', *British Journal of Educational Psychology*, vol. 46, 1976.

Miller, C. M. L., and Parlett, M., *Up to the Mark* (Society for Research in Higher Education, 1974).

Moodie, G. C., and Eustace, R., *Power and Authority in British Universities* (Allen & Unwin, 1974).

Neave, G., 'Academic drift: some views from Europe', *Studies in Higher Education*, vol. 4, no. 2, October 1979.

Nuffield Group for Research and Innovation in Higher Education, *Newsletters*, nos 1–7, *The Drift of Change* (Interim Report), 1975, *Making the Best of It* (Final Report), 1976 (Nuffield Foundation, 1972–6).

Östergren, B., and Berg, B., *Innovations and Innovation Processes in Higher Education* (Swedish National Board of Universities and Colleges, 1977).

Packwood, T., 'The school as a hierarchy', *Educational Administration*, vol. 5, no. 2, Spring 1977.

Parlett, M., *et al.*, *Learning from Learners* (Nuffield Foundation, 1976).

Parlett, M., and Dearden, G. (eds), *Introduction to Illuminative Evaluation: Studies in Higher Education* (Pacific Soundings Press, 1977).

Pask, G., 'Styles and strategies of learning', *British Journal of Educational Psychology*, vol. 46, 1976.

Pateman, T. (ed), *Counter Course: A Handbook for Course Criticism* (Penguin, 1972).

Perry, W. G., Jnr, *Forms of Intellectual and Ethical Development in the College Years* (Holt, Rinehart & Winston, 1970).

Pike, R. S., McIntosh, N. E. S., and Dähllof, U., *Innovation in Access to Higher Education* (International Council for Educational Development, 1978).

Pinker, R. A., *Social Policy and Social Theory* (Heinemann, 1971).

Platt, J., *Realities in Social Research: An Empirical Study of British Sociologists* (Sussex University Press, 1976).

Price, Don K., *The Scientific Estate* (Harvard University Press, 1965).

Premfors, R., and Östergren, B., *Systems of Higher Education: Sweden* (ICED, 1978).

Pronay, N., 'Towards independence in learning history', *Studies in Higher Education*, vol. 4, no. 1, March 1979.

Reid, W., and Epstein, L., *Task Centred Casework* (Columbia University Press, 1972).

Reid, W., and Shyne, A., *Brief and Extended Casework* (Columbia University Press, 1969).

Report of the William Tyndale Junior and Infants School Public Inquiry (the Auld Report) (ILEA, 1976).

Riley, Judith, 'Course teams at the Open University', *Studies in Higher Education*, vol. 1, no. 1, March 1976.

Robinson, E., *The New Polytechnics* (Penguin, 1968).

Sheldrake, P., and Berry, S., *Looking at Innovation: Two Approaches to Educational Research* (NFER, 1975).

Snyder, B. R., *The Hidden Curriculum* (Knopf, 1971).

SSRC, *Health and Health Policy, Priorities for Research, Appendix III, Concepts of Health and Illness* by Margaret Stacey (SSRC, 1977).

Startup, R., 'Material resources and the academic role', *Studies in Higher Education*, vol. 4, no. 2, October 1979.

Swedish National Board of Universities and Colleges, *Research into Higher Education: Processes and Structures*, report from a conference in June 1978.

Tapper, Ted, and Salter, Brian, *Education and the Political Order* (Macmillan, 1978).

Thomas, R. E., 'Corporate strategic planning in a university', unpublished paper given at a seminar, 'Politics of higher education', International Political Science Association and SSRC, Paris, 1978.

Thompson, M., 'Class, caste, the curriculum cycle and the cusp catastrophe', *Studies in Higher Education*, vol. 1, no. 1, March 1976.

Trow, M., 'Reflections on the transition from mass to universal higher education', *Daedalus*, vol. 99, 1970.

Trow, M., 'The public and private lives of higher education', *Daedalus*, vol. 104, Winter 1975.

Trow, M., 'The American academic department as a context for learning', *Studies in Higher Education*, vol. 2, no. 2, March 1976.

University of Birmingham, *Report of the Review Body Appointed by the University* (the Grimond Report) (University of Birmingham, 1972).

University of Oxford, *Report of Commission of Enquiry* (the Franks Report), Vol. 1 (Oxford University Press, 1966).

Webb, Adrian, 'Social service administration: a typology for research', *Public Administration*, vol. 49, Autumn 1971.

Whitburn, J., Mealing, M., and Cox, C., *People in Polytechnics: A Survey of Polytechnic Staff and Students 1972–3* (Society for Research in Higher Education, 1976).

Williams, G., *et al.*, *The Academic Labour Market: Economic and Social Aspects of a Profession* (Elsevier, 1974).

Zinberg, D. S., 'Education through science: the early stages of career development in chemistry', *Social Studies of Science*, vol. 6, 1976.

Index

(See also references in Notes and Bibliography)

quinquennial grant system, 40

radio astronomy, 103
Regional Advisory Councils, 20, 21, 50, 168
research
balance in relation to teaching, 34, 81, 103, 108–9
connections with tenure, 105
councils, 34, 35, 52, 99
sponsorship of, 52–3
research-based units, 80–85
researchers, full-time, 107
temporary, 105, 107–8
reward systems, 69
Robbins Committee and Report (1973), 35, 42, 47, 49, 122
and CNAA, 38
on objectives of higher education, 45–6
principle of open access, 41
Roscoe, Henry, 39
Rothschild Report, 53
Royal College of Physicians, 84
Royal Colleges, 161, 194
Royal Commissions on Universities, 39, 47
Royal Institute of Chemistry, 83
Royal Society, 83, 161

salary scales
made uniform, 33
of academics, 24, 36
sandwich courses, 135
Scottish universities
Royal Commission on, 39
structures of, 67
secondary school teaching
administrative structure, 196–7
evaluation of, 195
examinations, 209 n.19
modes of, 190
pastoral system, 190
peer group system, 190–91
secretarial services, 175
senates, 68, 69, 77
Snyder, B., 6
social work
evaluation of, 195
levels of, 187
working modes of, 190
St. Andrews University, 39
staff
and basic units, 102, 105
appointments of, 66
assessment of, 207 n.5
associations of, 48
development programmes, 129
non-professorial, 130–32
salaries, 203 n.21
staffing ratios (1939–1957), 30, 34

standards
academic, 31, 169–70
changes in, 32–5
state
role of the, 26, 38, 43, 47
UGC's views on support from the, 40
see also grants
students
and assessments, 157–8, 113–14
as social beings, 115–17
counselling, 129
initiation of changes, 137–8
learning styles, 112
numbers of, 1, 28, 29, 32, 35, 42, 100–01, 106, 126
prospectuses produced by, 158
reactions to assessment, 113–14
relations with teachers, 116–17
their studies, 112
uprisings 1968, 129
student unions, 117–18, 205 n.11
Sussex University
collegial structure of, 67
creation of, 34
Swedish higher education, 1, 18
universities, studies of, 121
U68 reforms, 144–5
central authorities, 204 n.5, 205 n.14

Taylor Report on School Government, 198
teacher training, closure and merger of institutions of, 51, 126
teaching
assessment of, 156, 160
extension of range in polytechnics, 123
necessity for and status of, 105–7, 193
technical colleges, 36
technical education council (TEC), 22
technological universities, 29, 34, 47
technology, status of, 84
tenure and reward systems, 68
theology, 24, 134
Treasury
expenditure and grants from, 47, 61
transfer of functions from, 42
trend to voluntary staying on at school, 35
Tyndale, William, School Inquiry, 197

Ulster, University of, 67
universities
and central authorities, 20
and higher education, 29
civic, 67
establishment of new, 122–3
federal, 67
origins of, 37